MEMORY MAKERS

James T. Covert, Ph.D.   **Jan S. Smith, Ph.D.**

Cover & Illustrations by Peter Cook

Frank Amato Publications
Portland, Oregon 97202
503-658-8108

To
Tom, Jake, Sally, Marcus,
Michael, Jennifer, Juliann,
Elizabeth, Christine and
our parents

Contents

Chapter Two: Vacations 41

Chapter Three: Holidays 67

Chapter Four: School Days 94

Chapter Five: Fun with Food 119

Chapter Six: Special Occasions

Conclusion

Introduction

I t can be said that the problem with childhood is that it passes by too quickly, and that we, as adults, remember too few of the happy moments we had during this period of our lives.

Most of the important memories we retain from our childhood are centered around the family. Perhaps there was an extra special family vacation that today brings a smile to our faces every time we think of it. Or maybe there was a card game that became a family favorite during the holidays. Or possibly we might remember the simplest of things, such as Mom adding green food coloring to our mashed potatoes on St. Patrick's Day.

Memory Makers is a book written to help adults create cherished family moments . . . the kind of moments that can help build a strong and everlasting family bond. Additionally, ideas in this book can help teach you how to develop, within your children, an appreciation of family heritage and tradition. This book also includes ideas that can help your family members have fun while they learn, and learn while they have fun.

Memory Makers will also give you ideas on how to preserve all these wonderful memories so that your children will be able to look back upon them in greater detail. This book will give you ideas on how to record special family events in an organized fashion, using 35 mm cameras, instant cameras, audio cassette recorders, video cameras, photograph albums and montages, and diaries.

There are more ways to preserve family memories today than at any time in history. The family's ability to preserve memories took a giant leap forward with the development of video cameras, for example. Additionally, 35 mm and instant cameras are increasingly advanced and easier to use. Audio cassette recorders are smaller, easier to use, and more reliable than ever. And there are also excellent photo albums and other organizational tools to help families preserve memories.

The problem seems to be that many families aren't organized enough to fully utilize the technology that's available. Photographs are thrown into shoe boxes and get lost in closets and attics. Videotapes are accidentally recorded over. And audio cassette tapes are seldom thought of or used.

A major focus of *Memory Makers* is to help families create memorable events that can be preserved. Along with these suggestions, this book offers ways to organize these memories so that they are easily stored, logically arranged, and fun to look at. A family with a plan for preserving an event will take more care to obtain the desired photographs, postcards, or audio tapes . . . and will be more satisfied with the results.

Video Cameras

If you already own one of these, you know how wonderfully easy they are to use, and how portable they are. The newer video camcorders, with the recorder incorporated right into the camera, are preferred for their light weight and because it is not necessary to carry the recorder around as a separate unit.

Look for simplicity in the camera and ask about lighting ranges. You'll want to be able to shoot in various lighting conditions. Automatic focus is as important a feature as automatic zoom.

When shooting, what you see and hear is what you get. However, video buffs may want to edit what they've shot into a more polished product. A good video store can direct you to a company that can help you accomplish this.

An idea that is popular is to have still photographs transferred to video, and then add music and narration. This allows you to create your own customized television program starring your family!

Remember, it is vitally important to label all videotapes and store them upright in a cool environment. Doing so will make for many years of family viewing pleasure.

Audio Cassette Recorders

Today, audio cassette recorders are so lightweight and small, that you can easily store them in a shirt pocket.

Audio cassette recorders are especially good to use around young children who are just learning how to talk. The sound of their sweet little voices will bring a lot of happiness to your family in years to come.

Audio cassette recorders are also an excellent item to bring along during family reunions. Children and parents can interview grandparents about their early lives, and transcribe this information for later use in developing a family tree.

As with videotapes, audiotapes should be carefully labeled and stored in a cool environment.

Photographs

We recommend that, whenever possible, two types of cameras be used when taking pictures. The first is an instant camera, which will guarantee that you have a visual record of a particular event, just in case your 35 mm photographs don't turn out properly. The second is a 35 mm camera which will provide your family with professional, detailed photographs which will last a lifetime. You may wish to take pictures in both color and black and white, the latter of which provide a wonderful "archival" look to your family albums.

Anytime your family goes on an outing, be sure to bring the cameras along. You never know when a great photo opportunity will present itself. And bring along plenty of film and batteries. You may be able to save about half of the cost of film if you buy it in bulk at large discount stores. Be sure to check the expiration date on all film which you purchase.

Photographs should always be dated, and whenever possible, you should write a little something about what's in the picture, directly on the back of the photograph.

We recommend asking for double prints whenever you have film developed. The first set of prints should go in the family album, or in family picture frames. The second set of prints can be divided among grandparents and children, all of whom will cherish their own copies.

It's a good idea to invest in sturdy photo albums which will be able to stand the test of time. Keep the photo albums in a place where your children can look at them often. When they do so, you can help them remember events by reminiscing with them.

Diaries

A family diary will be a real family treasure for generations to come. Keep it in a special, easily accessible place, so that even the youngest of family members can reach it, and write in it.

You will need to encourage family members to write in the family diary on a regular basis. Perhaps you can choose a particular time of day or week when entries should be made. Naturally, you will want to date all entries, and have family members sign their names after everything they choose to write in the family diary.

Personal diaries can also be kept by family members. Your children will probably want a lock and key for theirs, which is perfectly understandable. Children need privacy at times, and their personal diaries are an excellent place to start.

We hope you will find *Memory Makers* to be a valued family resource of ideas, activities and events which can enhance your family experience and create lasting memories for everyone in your family. Some of the ideas are designed to promote learning or family heritage. Others are suitable as yearly "just-for-fun" traditions that can be passed down from generation to generation. Others offer unique ways to add fun and memories to family holidays and vacations. For many of the Memory Maker suggestions in this book, you may wish to customize the activities to suit your own family's needs. We think this is a great idea!

The years when your family is together as a cohesive unit are the most important years for the development of your children's character. When you think about it, you only have about ten years (when your children are between the ages of about three and thirteen) to instill in them a "feeling of family."

So take full advantage of this time to plan quality events and activities which will give your children roots as well as wings.

With trends toward two-career families and one-parent families, the time spent with our children is more limited, and consequently, more important than ever. It is our hope that this book will help you, as parents and grandparents, make the best use of this time.

We hope *Memory Makers* will help you create, for you and your children, memories of some of the most delightful and heart-warming moments of your lives.

And don't be surprised if your children pass these wonderful Memory Makers on to their own children.

. . . And so on. And so on. And so on.

Happy reading, and happy memories!

James T. Covert, Ph.D.
Jan S. Smith, Ph.D.

Chapter One: Family Fun

We often talk about the "responsibility" of raising a family in grim tones. Certainly, raising a family is serious business that should not be taken lightly. But this doesn't mean it has to be a somber experience. In fact, many of the important lessons a parent can pass on are best received by a child who is in a receptive mood. And the most receptive mood often occurs when the child is having fun!

The "Family Fun" section of *Memory Makers* offers some suggestions on ways to disguise important values, traditions and lessons as "fun" activities. Some, such as "Family Portraits," "Snap that House," and "Family Monopoly," will promote in your children an appreciation of family unity. Others, like "Family Tree," "Family Stationery," and "Family Trivial Pursuit," will help build family pride and a sense of tradition. Still others, such as "Pet Pals" and "Adopt a Zoo Animal," will promote a sense of responsibility. So, go ahead! Have fun with these ideas!

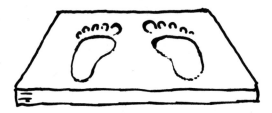

1. Footprints in the Cement

The next time your family prepares to move into a new house, be sure to be there the day the cement is poured for the sidewalk or the driveway.

Gather together all family members and before the cement dries, have everyone put his or her handprint and/or footprint in the cement. An adult can carefully write the family names under each print, and date this wonderful work of art. Children will delight in comparing how much their hands and feet have grown over the years!

In the absence of freshly poured cement, handprints and footprints can be made in clay, on paper with fingerpaints, or in Christmas cookie dough, and baked. Don't forget to label and date them!

2. Family Portraits

Let's face it, parents love family portraits a lot more than kids do. But, the funny thing about kids is that they soon grow up to be adults, and then they seem to love the old photographs of the family even more than their parents do! So, snap away! Kids may grumble a bit today, but down the road, they're going to love these dated family snapshots.

If possible, enroll your family in a professional portrait program offered by a local photography studio. That way, you will receive yearly reminders when it is time to come in again. Try framing a single family portrait, or a montage of individual portraits taken of each family member.

Family portraits taken at home should include traditional poses of the family sitting around the fireplace or on the couch, and an additional pose of everyone standing in a group pose. Kids will get a kick out of doing height comparisons as they browse through the portraits in years to come.

3. Photo Albums

A great way to help children appreciate family photographs is to give each child a photo album of his or her own.

When having photographs from birthday parties, vacations, Christmas, or other special occasions developed, ask for double prints, which usually cost just pennies more each. Keep one full set for the family album, and then divide the duplicates evenly among the children. Not only will the children be able to take pride in their own photo albums, they also will have something very sentimental to take with them when they go to college, move out of the house, or get married.

Children should be encouraged to write little notes by the pictures in their albums. This will help them remember people and events better. And, as always with photographs, show the children how to date the photos on the back by simply writing the day, month and year.

4. Snap that House

Every year, on the first day of Spring, children will look forward to an activity called "Snap that House."

Start off the day with some serious Spring cleaning, in which all family members participate. Then, buy a new roll of film with 24 or 36 exposures. Divide the number of available shots by the number of family members old enough to operate a camera. Kids will love this!

Let's say you purchase a roll of film with 24 shots, and you have six family members. Each family member will get to take any four shots of the house, inside or out. Parents should take shots of things the children might miss, like the baby's room, the den, the kitchen or the garage. All developed photographs should then be placed in a special album. This will give children lasting memories of the various places in which they grew up. They will especially enjoy looking at shots of their old bedrooms!

5. Matching T-Shirts

Kids love T-shirts! They also love to feel grown-up. Well, here's a great way to combine both of these loves and thrill the kids, too!

Let's say you have two children. And let's say Mom went to college at the University of Oregon, and Dad went to college at Notre Dame. Next Christmas, write away to your alma maters and order "Duck" and "Fighting Irish" T-shirts in your sizes and your children's sizes. Your kids will feel so "cool" wearing college T-shirts like yours!

One of the best times for your family to wear these shirts is when you attend a sporting event at one of the colleges, or watch it on television.

You and your children will also enjoy wearing T-shirts from the closest professional sports teams. This is big-league fun for the kids! Remember to take pictures of the whole family decked out in matching T-shirts.

6. Name Your Car

A child delights in saying to a friend, "We took Susie to Disneyland last week." And the friend will say, "Who's Susie?" And the child will say, "Our CAR!" Kids love to name cars. They also love to name their homes, their bicycles, their pets, and their toys.

When it comes to naming your home, you can select an interesting name that best represents your house. You can use this name on your family stationery, refer to it when giving directions, and even have the name put on a plaque over your street address on the front of your residence. This is a tradition still used in other countries, and dates back to medieval times when residences were owned by gentry and aristocrats.

Naming cars, homes, bicycles, pets and toys encourages children to be creative, playful and fun-loving. They'll also take better care of their things if they give them names first.

7. Backyard Theatre

Encouraging your children to stage "Off-Off Broadway" productions in your backyard will lead to lasting memories for you and your little actors. This is a photo or video opportunity which should not be missed!

Children should write their own plays and make their own costumes. They may choose to write plays based on books they have read or stories they have heard. Once scripts have been written, the children should make copies for all the "actors," who can be siblings or neighborhood friends.

Children should rehearse the plays until they are ready to "go public." Then, they may give tickets to the neighbors, or sell tickets for a penny, or a nickel or a dime. As in real theatre, there should be an intermission, during which the children may offer lemonade. After the play is over, the children will be filled with pride. At breakfast the next day, present the children with a written "review" of their wonderful performances!

8. Family Monopoly

Here's an activity suited for older children.

Children and parents who like "arts and crafts" projects, can build a "Family Monopoly Board." This can be done by using everything from cardboard to real wood. Your Family Monopoly Board should look like a real Monopoly board; however, all properties should be renamed with street names or family names familiar to the children.

Play money can be homemade or purchased inexpensively at a variety store. Playing pieces can be lucky charms, lucky coins, or any number of very small toys found around the home. Houses and hotels can be made out of clay and painted. The board should be painted in bright colors.

This is guaranteed to be a lot of fun, both to make and to play. Sturdy Family Monopoly boards can be used over and over again.

9. Pet Pals

Pets are an important part of children's lives. Sometimes children realize the true meaning of love as the result of caring for a pet. And in most cases, children have some of the most fun and most tender moments of their lives with their pets. Dogs, cats and horses make particularly good pets, but even goldfish can add a lot of sparkle to a child's life.

If possible, pets should be adopted from the local Humane Society. This provides an excellent opportunity for children to learn about adoption, pet overpopulation, and how to care for small animals.

Make sure your child feeds, grooms, plays with, and cleans up after the pet. Take your child to the library and read books together that explain proper pet care procedures. And, above all, understand that your child will develop a great attachment to the pet. A gift of a special photograph of your child with the pet will be a present long treasured by your child.

10. Family Stationery

Children can be taught very early in life to take pride in their family name. One way to foster such pride is to design your own family stationery.

The stationery, which can be printed inexpensively at a local print shop, should include your family's name and address, and, if you wish, your family's crest or a special logo your family designs together. The letterhead stationery and envelopes should be treated as "special," and children should be allowed to use them only when they write special letters.

Thank-you letters and other special occasion letters to grandparents and relatives should be written by the children on their family stationery. Letters to Santa Claus, the President of the United States, and other important people in your children's lives can also be written on the family stationery.

11. The Family Diary

Keeping a family diary is a fun and simple way to teach children how to preserve the present. It will also be great fun for them to read as they grow older.

Each family member, including parents, should write a few lines in the family diary each day or week. Younger children, not yet able to write, should be encouraged to draw a picture, or scribble!

The family diary can be kept in a loose-leaf notebook. Entries should be dated and signed. Entries can include notes about family activities, school activities, special events, the weather, pets, friends, or anything about which family members would like to write a couple of sentences.

Remember, a few lines written in the family diary each day by one or more members of the family, is all it takes to provide your family with a valuable resource that will mean so much in years to come.

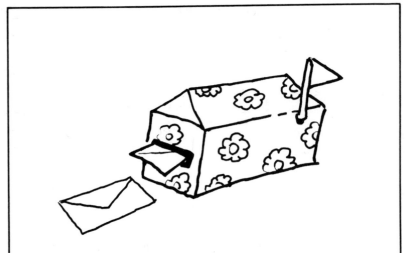

12. Letter Boxes

Here's a great family activity that will give both children and parents memories to last a lifetime.

Provide an empty shoebox for each member of the family. Then all family members can decorate their boxes in any way they wish. Parents should provide felt pens, crayons construction paper, scissors, glue, and any other arts and crafts material available around the home. Each decorated box should include the name of the family member.

Your children should find a special place for their own boxes, such as on their nightstands or in their drawers, or in the family library.

Children should be instructed to fill the boxes with all letters and cards they receive over the years. The key to this activity's success is to save and date all letters and cards, and treat them as private property.

13. Baby Books

Many parents feel that one of the most treasured gifts they can ever give a child is a baby book chronicling the child's first year of life.

Baby books can be purchased at stationery stores or department stores, or you can make your own version out of loose-leaf binders. The important thing is to chronicle all special events and interesting details regarding the first year of life for each of your children.

Be sure to include a photograph or two of your newborn. Hospital volunteers usually take pictures of newborns on the baby's first day or two of life, but family members can also take pictures. Baby books should also include notes about when the babies first opened their eyes, when they first smiled, when they first rolled over, when they spoke their first words, and what those words were, when they first tried solid food, when they got their first tooth, and when they first crawled and walked.

14. Family Tree

The first step in helping children understand their family tree can be taken by trying the following activity.

Using a map of the United States or the world, note the cities or geographical areas associated with your family's history. Assign different colors to paternal and maternal branches. Draw dots where relatives lived and lines where various ancestors or relatives traveled over the years. This map can either be framed or tacked to the wall.

Once children have a sense of where their relatives once lived, it is easier for them to understand a "family tree." Trace back as far as your children's great grandparents and draw a simple family tree. As the children grow older, names of great-great grandparents and great-great-great grandparents should be added to the family tree. You may also wish to invest in having a professional genealogist help trace your family tree.

15. Family Reunions

Family reunions are a great time to ask relatives to fill out family tree questionnaires about their lives and their relatives. But, most of all, family reunions should be a time of great fun and lasting memories for you and your children.

One way to help your children really look forward to family reunions is to arrange with favorite relatives to serve as your children's special friends. For example, if you have a 10-year-old daughter, she may really enjoy spending some time at the reunion with an 18-year-old cousin who is in college. It will make your daughter feel grown-up, and will make her feel like the family reunion is really special. Months before the family reunion, encourage your daughter and her cousin to begin writing letters. It will be such a treat for the two of them to see each other when the family reunion finally arrives. This also serves to link your family with your relatives' families, and to link the past to the present and the future.

16. Family Coat-of-Arms

Many families have an authentic coat-of-arms, but most do not. If your family is among those which do not, you can design your own, and pass it on for generations to come.

It's easy to make a family coat-of-arms. First of all, your family should look at some library books on the topic of heraldry to see what the coat-of-arms of other families look like.

Then your family should agree on the colors it likes best, and perhaps a basic idea, goal or theme that your new coat-of-arms should have. Then give each member of the family some paper, colored pencils, crayons and felt pens, and let them try to design your new coat-of-arms. Your family should decide which design it likes best. Then someone in your family who is skilled in woodcarving, or a professional woodcarver, can make a shield with your coat-of-arms on it for your family room wall.

17. All Aboard!

One thing children will likely remember for a lifetime is a trip across the country on a train. This makes for a wonderful experience for children as young as five years old. Start off with a few short trips to neighboring cities, and if your children take to the rails, try this week-long adventure!

Sleeping compartments, which can accommodate up to six family members, offer great excitement for children on trains. Small children can fit two to a bed, and even have room left over for a teddy bear or two.

Cross-country train trips can offer children their first opportunity to collect small souvenirs. Items such as maps, flags, patches and postcards can be collected by your children at various whistle-stops. These small souvenirs are the makings for scrapbooks which your children can make with a little help from you. A photograph of your family with the conductor of the train also makes a nice addition to the scrapbooks.

18. Safe Deposit Box

A family safe deposit box provides the opportunity for children to learn the meaning of the word "valuable."

Your children will delight in having the opportunity to accompany you to the bank. If your children receive savings bonds for their birthdays or on holidays, they will enjoy coming with you to the bank to put the savings bonds away in the family safe deposit box.

Your children might also enjoy seeing some of the other "secret" items you have in the box, such as coins, your marriage certificate, their birth certificates, and parents' wills, in which bequests for treasured items can be made to each of your children. Seize this opportunity to teach your children about the importance of keeping secret the contents of your family safe deposit box. Your children will soon take great pride in sharing with you the secrets of this family treasure.

19. Backyard Campouts

It's not necessary to take your family into the backwoods in order to hear scary things that go bump in the night!

A tent, some sleeping bags, a couple of flashlights and some vivid imaginations are all that are needed to give children a real camping-out experience right in your own backyard.

You can make these campouts especially memorable by providing some of the children's favorite munchies, and by telling a story or two about the great outdoors! Boys seem to really love camping out in the backyard with their fathers, and girls seem to enjoy camping out with their mothers. But, whoever the campers might be, they are sure to appreciate their own warm beds the next night!

Hot chocolate with marshmallows is a must the following morning!

20. Adopt a Zoo Animal

If you live anywhere near a zoo, here's an idea you might want to consider.

Many large zoos have an adopt-a-zoo-animal program. Families who make a small donation ($5-$100), can adopt a zoo animal, and receive adoption papers! Naturally, the adopted zoo animal continues to live at the zoo, but your children will enjoy their visits to the zoo even more, knowing they are the proud "parents" of one of the animals.

This will provide you with an excellent opportunity to foster your children's natural curiosity about wild animals. You may wish to explore the possibility of enrolling your children in summer zoo camps, or accompany your children to the library to read books about the type of zoo animal the family has adopted. Be sure to take a picture of your zoo adoptee and include it in the family picture album.

21. Baseball, Mom & Apple Pie

What could be more wholesome than baseball, mom and apple pie? And what three things evoke such warm memories, long into adulthood? Well, here's a way to combine all three, and treat your children to something they will look forward to year after year.

At least once a season, pack up the whole family in the car and take them to a ballgame. Major league baseball is certainly the most thrilling, but AAA games, college games or even high school games can get the old hearts pumping, too! Mom, Dad, and all the kids should come along, and a sweet surprise of apple pie can be promised for everyone after the game.

Making this a yearly tradition is the key. If your family loves the Dodgers, for example, take them out to the ballgame every year for the opening game. When the game is over, you can all have hot apple pie a la mode. Year after year, your children will look forward to this!

22. The Family Hammock

Any child who has grown up with a hammock in the backyard, knows the joy of swaying back and forth in total comfort, staring at the clouds drifting by. A person in a hammock hasn't a care in the world!

A hammock is one of those things that a family really doesn't need until it gets one. Then it becomes an absolute necessity!

In the summertime, Mom and Dad can sway back and forth together in a securely tied hammock, while the children play underneath in the shade. You will find that a hammock can sway away even the most stressful worries. Truly, the family that sways together, stays together!

And don't worry if your backyard doesn't have two sturdy trees from which to suspend a hammock. You can purchase a freestanding hammock at many of the same places at which outdoor furniture is sold.

23. Measuring Up

Many families keep track of the height measurements of their children by making small pencil marks on kitchen door-jams or hall archways every year. This is a clever way to have children visualize how fast they are growing, but it is a record of their heights that is not transportable should your family move!

An easy way to overcome this dilemma is to purchase a wide board (1 inch x 10 inches x 7 feet), paint or varnish it, and let it become your measurement record for all of your children.

Dated measurements can be drawn right on this easily stored board, and your children can pass the board along to the next generation.

From your children's first birthdays to their twenty-first birthdays, take measurements every year, and watch them grow up, up and away!

24. Family Trivial Pursuit

Here's a fun activity that helps children learn about their parents' lives, and helps them remember their own lives, too!

Family Trivial Pursuit is a great game to play on the first day of winter each year. All you'll need is a regular Trivial Pursuit game, and some heavy paper stock to add your own family questions. You'll notice that Trivial Pursuit cards include several categories of questions, such as "Science," "History," and "Literature." Parents can personalize the game by creating 100 or so questions and answers about all members of the family. Then, when a player lands on a "History" question, a "family" history question can be substituted for the regular Trivial Pursuit "History" question.

Questions about Mom, for example, might include: "From which college did Mom graduate?" "In what year was Mom born?" "What was Mom's grandmother's name?" And, "What was Mom's maiden name?"

25. Go Fly a Kite

Sometimes it just seems like spring hasn't arrived until you see children flying kites!

Your family might want to consider making and flying kites an annual ritual. You can make those rainy days of March perk right up by getting the whole family involved in preparing kites. Lots of fun will be had by all if you make your own kites, either from kits or from scratch!

Be creative! Use bright colors and unusual shapes. Kids seem to love box kites and kites which look like exotic animals! And, since kites have a knack of crashing, be sure to take photographs as your children are making their kites, and as they send them up into the sky for the very first time. Remember . . . stay away from trees and sources of electrical power.

This is the kind of fun kids remember year after year!

26. Family Table Cloth

Your family can cover a lot with its own family table cloth.

The next time your family gathers at a reunion or a special event, such as a wedding, have each family member sign a specially purchased white table cloth. Use an indelible pen, or several indelible pens in assorted colors.

Each family member might add a comment about themselves, the event, or the family. Children can draw a picture after their names. Perhaps they will enjoy drawing a picture of the event which has brought your family together on this occasion. Parents can add the date to the table cloth.

Once the event is over and all have gone their way, your family will have a white table cloth decorated with family names and remarks. This family table cloth is something that can be treasured and passed on to other family members for generations to come.

27. Family Flag

One great way to show that your family is flying high with pride is to design and sew your own family flag.

All that is needed is a flag pole in your yard, or one attached to your house or apartment. The family flag is something which can be flown on special family days, such as birthdays, anniversaries and graduations. In addition, the family flag can be flown on days when no one in the family has to do chores. (Now, that's a special occasion!)

If you have a family coat-of-arms or family crest, it will be easy to adapt its symbol to the design of your family flag. If you don't already have a coat-of-arms or family crest, simply have your children help you create a flag, choosing colors and symbols that have special meaning to your family. Your children and your neighbors will enjoy seeing your family flag fly! And don't forget to bring along the family flag to picnics, the beach or campgrounds, where it can serve to mark your family's spot.

28. Family Slide Shows

If you have several children in your family, you may have encountered some difficulty in having them all sit comfortably around the family photo album. Helping everyone see the same pictures all at once is no small task. Luckily, there is a way to overcome this problem by having periodic family slide show nights.

Although your neighbors may not find your family slides very interesting, your children certainly will, especially if you include your children's faces in as many of your shots as possible! Naturally, as your children grow older, they will really enjoy seeing the family's older slides, when they, and you, were much younger. But, whether the family slide show includes new or old slides, this can be a time of tremendous fun and laughter for all family members.

Kids will really love family slide show night if you darken the room and serve hot popcorn, just like at the movies!

Chapter Two: Vacations

With careful planning, vacations can be special times when Mom, Dad and the kids can share new experiences. An important point to remember when planning your family vacations is that everyone will be taking part in the vacation, so it makes sense to plan the trip together, as a family. That way, Mom, Dad, and the kids can all say what they would like to get out of the vacation.

The preparation can also be helpful for parents wishing to incorporate some important family lessons into the trip. Planning to stop at historical markers along the way may take a few extra moments, but it may bring history to life for your children and spark an interest that wasn't there previously.

Likewise, a trip to a national monument, such as a volcano, may interest your children in geology. And a vacation centered around an activity such as skiing, boating or camping can promote an appreciation for recreational activities. If you plan carefully, vacations can be an ideal time to reinforce important values and to provide memorable experiences for your children—all while having a terrific time!

29. Souvenir Curio Cabinet

Vacation time is such a fun time for children, and bringing back souvenirs encourages the fun to live on in children's imaginations.

One problem with souvenirs is that they frequently get lost or misplaced. This problem can be easily overcome by having a family souvenir curio cabinet, in which small souvenirs from family vacations can be kept. These curio cabinets can be a dusting nightmare, but they're worth it!

Some of the items children delight in having as souvenirs are small polished rocks, dolls, glass or ceramic animals, bells, charms, flags, patches, shells, books, maps, and jewelry.

You might wish to prepare small captions for each of the souvenirs, making it easier to remember the vacations on which they were acquired.

30. Same Time, Next Year

If your family should hit upon a wonderfully successful vacation one year, you might want to consider this vacation as an annual outing.

One idea that really seems to please children is to attend the Grand Floral Parade every year in Pasadena. This requires a trip to Southern California on the day or two before New Year's Day. Many, many families camp out right on the sidewalk the night before the parade in order to ensure a good spot from which to watch the floats going by the following morning. Kids love this and will look forward to it year after year. Your children might also enjoy the Macy's Parade in New York City every year, or Mardi Gras in New Orleans. Or perhaps there is a special "festival" held in your area which your children will enjoy attending each year.

Another vacation which children love year after year is a trip to a ski resort during Christmas week. Just find an event that your children love, and you'll be amazed at how much they look forward to it each year!

31. Historical Markers

One way to keep children happily occupied in the car on long, driving vacations is to ask them to keep their eyes out for historical markers and to give them a chance to earn some souvenir cash in the process!

You might want to bring along a bag of shiny new dimes or quarters in the front seat. Then, every time one of the children spots an historical marker, that child and all your other children, too, each win a dime or quarter which they may spend on vacation souvenirs. This is a fun way to help spark children's interest in history and souvenir collecting.

When an historical marker is spotted, you might consider stopping the car and enjoying a brief historical lesson with the children. Bring along the camera, too, as photographs of historical markers make good additions to the family scrapbook. If your family is feeling really ambitious, you may want to write down some information about the historical site, and add new questions to your "Family Trivial Pursuit" game.

32. Vacation Diaries

Vacation diaries are something that children will get a kick out of making, and it will help keep memories of family vacations alive for many years to come.

For shorter vacations, children can simply write down impressions or describe events on common loose-leaf paper. Each child can capture the trip according to individual ability. Younger children might just draw pictures of their experiences. Older children might even write poems or songs about their trip. Save these entries for the family archives.

For longer vacations, you might want to purchase a bound book with blank pages. These can be found at stationery stores and bookstores. Children can take turns writing and drawing in the book while your family is on vacation. Parents can make entries, too! When you return home, the vacation diary will be a great addition to your family library.

33. Postcard Collections

There are lots of wonderful reasons for collecting postcards on family vacations, but there is one very practical reason for doing so. Postcards provide insurance just in case your vacation snapshots don't turn out! (Have you ever had vacation photographs developed only to discover that all of the pictures were overexposed or underexposed?)

That's the practical reason. Now the fun reason. Children love postcards. Some children like to collect them in a scrapbook. Others like to arrange them in a framed montage. Either way, there's lots of fun involved in teaching children how to properly mount their postcards and identify them.

And postcards are doubly fun when children collect a set for themselves, and send the rest to their friends and relatives. Be sure to bring along the names and addresses of the lucky recipients whenever you go on vacation!

34. Maps on Laps

When taking a long car trip, parents are certain to hear their children say, "How much longer until we get there?" Children without maps on their laps have been known to ask this question every five minutes.

There are two great ways to satisfy children's need to know, "How much longer?" One way is to provide all of your children with a map of their own. The other way is to provide each of your children with an inexpensive wristwatch.

Before leaving on vacation, you can call a family meeting, during which you can explain to the children where you are going on vacation, how long it will take to get there, and how to read their maps. Help the children mark the route you will be taking so they will be able to tell for themselves how much longer it will be until you get there! This also serves to help children remember where they went on vacation.

35. Car Games

Trips that require long hours in an automobile can be fatiguing for children as well as adults. But car games can make the time go by more quickly, and can provide laughter, amusement and memories for everyone.

The "A, B, C" game, for example, requires everyone to try to locate the letters of the alphabet sequentially, using signs along the road. If the situation becomes desperate, such as in wilderness areas, change the rules to include automobile license plates on passing cars.

The "Grocery Game" requires everyone to take turns naming items that can be found in the grocery store which begin with the letter "A," or "B," or "C," and so on. Using the letter "C," Mom might say "cabbage," Dad might say "cottage cheese," your daughter might say, "cotton balls," and your son might say, "Cheerios." Then, it's back to Mom, and Dad, and so on. The last person who can name a "C" grocery product wins the game.

36. World's Fair

The World's Fair comes to the United States or Canada every decade or so, and serves as an exciting opportunity for your children to meet people from around the world. Children will look forward to this once- or twice-in-a-lifetime treat with eager anticipation.

This international exhibition features exhibits and people from around the globe. It also has great rides for the children and delicious international cuisine for the whole family.

The World's Fair can serve as the site of a week-long vacation. Your family might enjoy renting a motor home and driving it to the Fair.

Children will be able to collect lots of free brochures from countries around the world. Pictures from these brochures can be placed in a scrapbook, and captions about various countries can be added.

37. Broadway

If your family is musically inclined, here's a vacation idea that you and your children will probably never forget.

When your children are teenagers, you might consider treating them to what may turn out to be their favorite vacation ever—a trip to Broadway! A good travel agent's help will be of considerable value.

Bring the family to New York for a two-, three-, or four-day vacation during which you all attend a Broadway musical. Choose lively musicals the whole family will enjoy, such as "Oklahoma," "My Fair Lady," or "Hello, Dolly!" To help your children enjoy and remember the musicals, purchase the records or cassettes before you see the shows, so they can listen to the music and sing along with the songs.

And while you're in New York, don't forget to visit the Statue of Liberty. It's a wonderful way to tell your children about our nation's cultural history.

38. Washington, D.C.

Children develop a sense of patriotism when they are very young. This sense of pride in their country can be further developed by taking them on a vacation to our nation's capital. It's a capital idea!

Before such a vacation is taken, you might wish to talk with your children's teacher about the kinds of things the children are studying in their classes relating to our nation's government. If your children are studying the White House, for example, they might enjoy taking a tour of it while visiting Washington, D.C. If they are studying Congress, they might enjoy watching Congress in session. And visits to the Washington Monument, the Lincoln and Jefferson Memorials, and the Smithsonian Institution will be unforgettable.

And your children can see the U.S. Constitution and the Declaration of Independence, both of which are on display in our nation's capital.

39. Disneyland

Every once in a while, your children might forget how to spell their own names, or they might forget what they had for breakfast, or they might forget what day of the week it is. But your children will never forget a trip to Disneyland (or Disney World).

There's a good reason why Disneyland is called the "Magic Kingdom." It's a place where children's dreams come true. It's fun and exciting and downright magical. It's a place where children can shake hands with Mickey Mouse, venture into uncharted waters with "Pirates of the Caribbean," explore the hair-raising thrills of outerspace flight on "Space Mountain," and discover that "It's a Small World" after all.

Bring along your camera, because your children will long cherish a photograph of themselves taken with Mickey, Minnie, Goofy, Snow White, Dopey, Donald Duck or any other of the characters they'll encounter.

40. Family Birthplaces

As your children grow older, they will develop a strong curiosity about where they were born and about where you were born. One way to satisfy this curiosity is to plan a vacation around visiting the birthplaces of all of your family members.

Not only will this be interesting to your children, it will also be interesting to you!

It's especially fun to visit the hospitals in which each member of your family was born. This provides parents with a wonderful opportunity to talk about how each child's birth brought such happiness to the family.

Side trips might also be taken to the places in which each family member lived as an infant. Old schools, old neighborhoods and old friends can also be visited. And since this is sometimes a once-in-a-lifetime vacation, be sure to take lots of pictures.

41. State Fairs

Your children will really look forward to taking a vacation to the State (or County) Fair each year if they are entered into one or more of the categories of competition.

As a family, you might wish to spend the year working on a family quilt which can be entered into the quilting competition. One type of quilt which would have special meaning to your family would be one on which squares were devoted to facets of your family's history.

Or, perhaps your children could raise something as small as a bunny or as large as a horse or cow. Competition in "animal" categories is great fun for children. And, if raising animals is out of the question, the children might like to spend the year perfecting a favorite family recipe, or growing roses which might walk away with a blue ribbon. Pick any category of competition that you know your children will enjoy, and watch your kids look forward to a family vacation at the State Fair each year!

42. Halls of Fame

A very memorable vacation can be made for your children by taking them to the Hall of Fame for their favorite sport. An example is given below for families which love baseball.

You might start off your vacation by visiting the Baseball Hall of Fame in Cooperstown, New York. There's plenty there to keep the children interested for hours! Be sure to point out some of the players that you really admired when you were a child.

Then take the children either to a spring training workout, or a regular season major league baseball game. Either one will be fun for your children. Spring training has the advantage of being less formal, which should give your children the chance to get a baseball autographed by all the players. A regular season game has all the great fans, the peanuts, the programs, the noise and the excitement!

43. Volcanoes

Here's a hot vacation idea that will burn brightly in your children's memories for many years to come.

Take a volcano vacation. Visit either Mt. St. Helens in Washington State or Mt. Kilauea on the Big Island of Hawaii. Both have exceptionally good tourism centers at which your family can learn about this most magnificent earthly phenomenon.

Volcanoes are something that have to be seen in person to be truly appreciated. Before taking a volcano vacation, you might want to go on a family outing to your local library in order to read about volcanoes. This will serve to enhance your children's appreciation of volcanoes when they later come face-to-face with one. Volcanoes are unbelievable sights to behold, and as such, you should bring your best camera along. If you get lucky, you'll get a shot of a plume of smoke or some molten lava.

44. College Campuses

Your teenagers may look forward to college with such excitement that they hardly take time to enjoy high school. Parents can share in this exciting time by planning a vacation around visiting college campuses.

Before embarking upon such a vacation, you may wish to spend some time with your teenager(s) at your city's main library, where you will probably find college catalogs from around the country. School counselors will also have college catalogs. Choose to visit colleges near home and away from home, with programs which cater to your child's interests.

Contact the colleges in advance, as they will be happy to arrange a tour for your entire family. Some colleges also make dormitory rooms available in the summer for a very reasonable nightly fee. A vacation of this sort is one which teens remember forever, and one which might very well serve to shape the course of their adult lives. For added fun, your family can pick up matching T-shirts at your teen's favorite college.

45. Sierra Club Trips

The Sierra Club, founded in 1892, is a nationwide organization with over 350,000 members. Each year, it sponsors about 300 trips to places throughout the United States, Canada, Mexico, and other parts of the world.

Sierra Club trips make great family vacations. If your family enjoys fishing, biking, hiking, skiing, river rafting, photography, and the great outdoors, you will find an ideal vacation waiting for you through the Sierra Club. Each trip is lead by naturalists and photographers who know the land well, and can teach your family about conservation.

Information about Sierra Club trips can be obtained by writing to the Sierra Club at 730 Polk Street, San Francisco, California 94109. You will receive information about trips, the teachers and the organization. And if your family is interested in participating in clean-up and restoration projects, including trail maintenance, you can go on special service trips for a minimal fee.

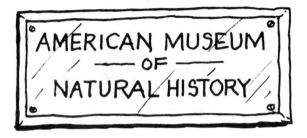

46. American Museum of Natural History

Throughout the year, the American Museum of Natural History, located in New York City, sponsors tours around the world. Each tour focuses on a particular aspect of natural history.

Information about these family vacation tours can be obtained by writing to the following address: American Museum of Natural History, Discovery Tours, Central Park West at 79th Street, New York, New York 10024. Prices vary for the trips, which include adventures in China, Africa, the Caribbean, Europe, and throughout the world.

These trips are led by noted scholars, who will be able to provide your family with background information and plenty of interesting stories. Though these trips are not recommended for families with small children, they are ideal for families with teenagers. The tours can make for memorable experiences for each member of your family, and can spark a real interest in natural history.

47. Cruises

Cruises have come a long way on their journey to please every member of the family. Nowadays, families can take cruises which are designed especially for families with children! You may be hard pressed to find another type of family vacation which is more memorable than a cruise!

Once your children reach elementary school, they will be old enough to appreciate the wonderful experience awaiting them on a cruise. The best way to make sure your family goes on the most ideally suited cruise is to visit your travel agent.

Many cruise ships offer supervised activities for children, all day long! That means that while your children are having the time of their lives, you and your spouse can have the time of your lives, too! Kids will be entertained with sports, arts and crafts, aerobics, and just about every other type of fun you can think of. And their cruise supervisors/teachers will bend over backwards to see that your children have a super time!

48. Assembly Line Vacation

The next time your family decides to buy a new American-made car, you might want to consider taking a family vacation to Michigan.

Your children will get a lot of pleasure out of seeing an automobile assembly plant for the very first time. Children can see how automobiles are made by taking any number of tours offered by selected plants. Typically, tours are given on one day each week, and are about two hours in length. Tour reservations can be obtained by writing to the automobile companies whose plants your family wishes to visit.

While in Michigan, you may also wish to take your family to the Henry Ford Museum located in Dearborn. Here, your children will be able to view a fascinating indoor collection of old cars, old airplanes and old trains. And, if you plan this vacation around the purchase of a new American-made car, the souvenir your family brings home will make this a vacation that will not soon be forgotten by your children or you!

49. See the Sea

A vacation during which your family visits the sea is one which will fill your children's minds with fascination and wonder for a long time to come. The fresh, cool sea air does a family good!

The great thing about vacations to the sea is that there is so much to do. These vacations provide a super opportunity for children to start sea shell collections. Children will enjoy cleaning the shells and mounting them on a piece of wood or making jewelry out of them.

Sea vacations might include trips to aquariums, sea otter caves, and whale watching. Children will also enjoy swimming, if the waters are safe and relatively warm. And most children will get a kick out of fishing, though most will not like being out in rough seas to do so! You might also want to bring along a book about birds, so that when your family spots interesting looking birds, you can take their pictures and identify them in your family vacation album.

50. State Capitols

A family vacation to your state capital is one which can be both educational and fun.

Before completing your plans for such a vacation, you might consider contacting your state representative. Ask if it would be possible for your family to meet him or her on your vacation. Most state representatives will be delighted to have the opportunity to say "hello" to their constituents and "future" constituents! If possible, take a picture of your children with the legislator from your district. And, who knows, your children may get lucky and get to have their pictures taken with the governor, too!

Your family will also enjoy taking a tour of the State Capitol Building, in which you will find many items of historical interest. You might want to bring along some watercolor paints and canvases, so your children can paint pictures of the Capitol. You can frame these pictures and later hang them in the children's rooms.

51. TV/Movie Vacation

A family vacation to Hollywood is one filled with cameras, lights and a whole lot of action.

Contact ABC, NBC and CBS before your vacation, in order to secure tickets to some of your favorite TV shows. (Out-of-town guests normally receive preferential treatment when it comes to doling out tickets.) If you can be a contestant on a game show, your children will remember this trip even more. NBC offers a terrific studio tour which your family should not miss!

Then it's off to the Universal Studios Tour, which your children will think is tops! They will get to see "Jaws" and all sorts of other scary and amazing things. They will see how movies are made, and, if they're lucky, even get to star in a mini-movie themselves!

In a word, a TV/movie vacation is just plain FUN!

52. Home Sweet Home

If there should come a year in your family's life in which no one can decide what to do on vacation, how about planning a vacation in your very own city?

It's amazing how much you will find to do right outside your doorstep. Your city may have its own historical society filled with interesting exhibits. Your city may also have a wonderful art museum, science museum or children's museum. And if you're lucky, there may be a zoo, too.

Are there movies playing right in town that your children have been longing to see? Have your children ever seen how the local newspaper is put together? They can take a tour of the local dairy, the local soft drink bottler's plant, the telephone company, the post office, the police station, the fire station and the city council chambers. And, how long has it been since the family spent the day at your local park? A wonderfully memorable vacation can be had right in your very own town!

53. Ski Vacation

Did you know that manufacturers make skis for children as young as two years old? So, bundle up your little ones (and your older children, too), and take the family on a ski vacation they will never forget!

Get a copy or two of a national ski magazine (which can be found right in your local grocery store), and read about ski resorts located near your home. There will be plenty of free brochures which you can write away for, and which will give you great ideas on how to make the most of a family ski vacation.

Ski lessons are offered at almost every ski resort in the nation. Your family will also be able to rent skis, boots, poles and bindings. Just dress everyone up warmly, and watch the good times roll! Children will long remember the cozy mountain cabins, the ski lifts, the snowmen, and the fun of it all. Start 'em while they're young, and this will be a family vacation they will look forward to winter after winter after winter!

Chapter Three: Holidays

Every holiday we celebrate exists for some reason. Some holidays are of religious origin, while others have historical or political importance. Holidays such as Mother's Day celebrate the family. And some, like Groundhog Day or April Fools' Day, exist mostly "just for the fun of it."

Because of their history and importance, holidays such as Christmas, Easter, Independence Day and Thanksgiving have strong cultural and family traditions tied to them. These holidays are important times for making memories and promoting values and traditions. A strong family tradition of events and activities during these holidays can help focus children's attention on your family's goals.

Other holidays can become special days with a little creativity and planning. Activities related to why the day is celebrated can help children understand more than the fact that the holiday means "no school."

Because there are already established traditions and family events around holidays, they are fertile ground for developing memories, strengthening values and reinforcing traditions. Be sure to take full advantage of these days!

54. New Year's Day

On this day, the earth begins another orbit around the sun, and in just 365 days, we earthlings will have travelled over 500 billion miles. New Year's Day, therefore, is a wonderful time of year to get out the family globe, and explain some of the wonders of the universe to your children.

The first day of January is also the time of year to make New Year's Resolutions. You might wish to encourage your children to write their resolutions down on a piece of paper, and then pin this list on their bedroom bulletin boards as a reminder.

Parents can be a terrific example to their children on this holiday by making and keeping New Year's Resolutions of their own. You can also use this holiday to not only get your finances in order, but to teach your children how to balance the budget and balance checkbooks. In this regard, you may wish to show your children how they can save a small amount of money each week, to accumulate a large amount by next New Year's Day.

55. Martin Luther King, Jr.'s Birthday

Martin Luther King, Jr. was born on January 15, 1929. In his lifetime, he became a noted civil rights leader, minister and recipient of the Nobel Peace Prize.

In the United States, his birthday is celebrated on the third Monday in January. On this day, you may wish to share books with your children about Dr. King's life, and the civil rights movement in the 1960s. Many television stations around the country also broadcast educational programs about Martin Luther King, Jr. on this day, and the programs often make excellent family viewing.

Parents can also help their children understand the importance of civil rights by conveying their feelings about growing up in the turbulent 1960s. You may wish to help your children write entries into their diaries on this day, in which they discuss their feelings about why civil rights are so important to people and families in this country.

56. Super Bowl Sunday

The world seems to come to a standstill on Super Bowl Sunday, so families might as well join in on this annual day of fun!

The game is especially fun if family members root for their favorite teams. Young children sometimes pick their favorite teams based on the color of the team's uniforms. That's okay!

You can add to your children's excitement by helping them to make pennants of their favorite teams, by using felt and felt pens. Attach the pennants to sticks, pencils or straws, and wave away. Of course, it will be helpful to explain the rules of football to your children so they will know when to cheer. And speaking of cheering, you'll hear a lot of that going on when you serve up traditional football fare on this day: hot dogs and hot chocolate! And, after the game, you'll be able to send away for the official Super Bowl program, which will make a great addition to your family scrapbook.

57. Groundhog Day

Most children will never see a groundhog on Groundhog Day, but this is still a holiday that can be quite memorable and fun for children.

First, your children will need to know the theory behind Groundhog Day. It is believed that if the sun shines, or the groundhog sees his shadow on February 2, then there will be six more weeks of winter. Groundhog Day, therefore, should be a day on which all children listen to the weather forecast for details about the next six weeks of weather.

And, if your family is anywhere near Punxsutawney, Pennsylvania on February 2, you can begin a Groundhog Day tradition by observing the annual Groundhog Day celebrations in this city. While there, you can visit Gobbler's Knob and Groundhog Zoo. If this sounds like a fun tradition in which your family can participate, write to: Chamber of Commerce, 123 S. Gilpin Street, Punxsutawney, Pennsylvania 15767 for more information. Who knows how much fun your family can have? The shadow knows!

58. Lincoln's Birthday

Abraham Lincoln, the sixteenth President of the United States, was born on February 12, 1809. He was assassinated while attending a performance of *Our American Cousin* at Ford's Theatre on April 14, 1865.

President Lincoln will be remembered most for his Emancipation Proclamation, his Gettysburg Address, his leadership during the Civil War and his proclamation establishing the last Thursday in November as Thanksgiving Day. Children remember that he was raised in a log cabin.

On his birthday each year, the family can start off the day by having pancakes with Log Cabin syrup. Later that evening, the family can build a log cabin with Lincoln Logs. Each year, make the log cabin bigger and better. Be sure to take a picture of the log cabin and the family each year, and include it in the family album. This is a tradition that children will pass on to their children, who will pass it on to their children, too!

59. Valentine's Day

St. Valentine's Day (February 14) is a special holiday for children. They will delight in exchanging Valentine's Day cards, flowers and chocolates.

You can make this holiday especially memorable for your children by making it a tradition in your family to make special, homemade valentines for each member of the family. Simply provide your children with red and white construction paper, red and white paper doilies, patterns of large, medium and small hearts, glitter, glue, scissors, and several narrow felt pens. Be sure to save all cards in your family scrapbook.

Children can also help decorate a Valentine's Day "tree" each year. Take a deadwood branch, about one foot in height, spray it white with Christmas tree flocking, and decorate it with hearts and cupids. This makes a nice centerpiece. For dessert, serve white cake cupcakes, with vanilla frosting and decorate them with cinnamon red hots! Pucker up!

60. George Washington's Birthday

George Washington was born on February 22, 1732. Celebrating his birthday each year can be great fun for children. No lie!

Since George Washington admitted to cutting down the cherry tree, it only seems right that families pay tribute to his honest character each year on his birthday by eating a cherry pie. If possible, get your children involved in the preparation of the cherry pie, as they will get a kick out of cooking something that smells so darn good coming out of the oven.

George Washington's Birthday is also an excellent holiday to help your children memorize the names of all the presidents of the United States, in the order in which they served. As your children grow older, you can also help them memorize something interesting about each president. Then, just for fun, each year have your children write a paragraph or two about what they would do if they were president. Keep all of these paragraphs in the family archives.

61. St. Patrick's Day

Children will enjoy celebrating the luck of the Irish each year on March 17, St. Patrick's Day. And, if your family happens to be Irish, be sure to spend a portion of the day talking with your children about their family heritage.

Each year on St. Patrick's Day, parents can give each child a lucky charm. Children are particularly fond of four-leaf clovers and wishbones.

Each St. Patrick's Day, help your children dress up in something green. Be sure the green is visible, so your children won't get pinched by their friends at school!

For dinner, serve Irish Stew with mashed potatoes. Add a few drops of green food coloring to the mashed potatoes in order to make them look especially lucky. Do the same with the children's milk. And don't forget to serve (green) chocolate chip mint ice cream for dessert!

62. April Fools' Day

April Fools' Day or All Fools' Day falls on April 1 of each year. Brady's *Clavis Calendaria,* 1812, says "The joke of the day is to deceive persons by sending them upon frivolous and nonsensical errands; to pretend they are wanted when they are not, or, in fact, any way to betray them into some supposed ludicrous situation, so as to enable you to call them 'An April Fool.' "

This is a particularly fun holiday for children who like to joke around. Parents can lead the way by playing harmless practical jokes on their children. You can start off the day by telling your children that it snowed overnight, and therefore school has been cancelled! April Fools'! Or you may wish to fill your children's closets with balloons, so they will break out in laughter when they go to open their closets. Children will also think it's funny when they discover that you have short-sheeted their beds, or placed several sheets of aluminum foil where their bottom sheet normally goes. Kids will always remember the fun they will have on this day!

63. Passover

One key to making Passover memorable for your children is to make this a hands-on holiday. There are so many fun activities for children on this holiday—activities that will keep them busy, while at the same time, help them understand the meaning of Passover.

Children can help you make the matzoh covers to be used at the family Seder (feast). You might choose to use white satin or muslin to form the seven-inch round or square covers. Children can help you embroider a Star of David on the covers. If you wish, the covers can be lined with plastic. Be sure to leave about one-third of the edge open on a round cover, or one side of a square cover open, so that the three pieces of matzoh can be inserted.

Children can also help set the table, decorate Seder plates, sing Passover songs, and search for the matzohs which you have hidden. You may also wish to reward them with prizes when they find the matzohs.

64. Easter Sunday

On this, the most joyous festival of the Christian year, children can participate in many delightful activities which they can pass on to their children someday.

The most traditional activity, of course, is the dyeing and decorating of Easter eggs. Children and adults of all ages enjoy coloring Easter eggs, and therefore, you should have plenty of eggs on hand. Parents can then hide the eggs, and children can hunt for them and fill their Easter baskets.

Children also love to make Easter egg trees. Hang a deadwood branch in a pot of clay, and paint it white, yellow and pink. Then poke a very small hole in each end of one dozen white eggs. Blow out the yolk and egg white from each egg. Then clean and dry the eggs. Your children can then paint the eggs with poster paint. Suspend the finished eggs from the deadwood branch using pastel-colored ribbons and bows.

65. May Day

The first day of May has been celebrated as a holiday since ancient times. It's a lovely day in the lives of children, who take great pleasure in making May Day baskets and giving them away.

During the months of March and April, you can save cottage cheese cartons, butter tubs and other food containers which would make nice baskets. On May Day, these containers can be covered with colored tissue paper or aluminum foil, and filled with Easter basket grass. A handle made of yarn or ribbon can be added, and then the basket can be filled with pretty flowers and small, wrapped candies. Once completed, your children can bring the baskets to neighbors' doorsteps, ring the doorbells and then run back home before they are spotted!

Children also enjoy making a special May Day basket for Mom each year, and placing it at her seat at the breakfast table before she gets up in the morning. This is a tradition that both the children and Mom will love.

66. Mother's Day

The second Sunday in May has been officially celebrated as Mother's Day since President Woodrow Wilson proclaimed it so in 1914. Your children will enjoy carrying on the tradition of honoring Mom, too.

Children can begin the day by serving Mom breakfast in bed. Dad or older siblings can supervise the preparations. Children can serve all of Mom's favorite foods. The breakfast tray might include a traditional rose in vase. Children can also make their own special Mother's Day cards which can be placed on the breakfast tray alongside the rose.

You can also make it a tradition in your family that on Mother's Day, Mom does no housework and no cooking. If possible, Dad and the children should take Mom out to dinner so there will be no chance of her getting stuck with doing the dishes! The next day, Mom can give each of the children a handwritten thank-you letter, in which she tells them how happy and proud she is to be their mother.

67. Memorial Day

On the last Monday in May, the people of the United States honor those who have died in service to our country. Memorial Day also serves as a day during which people pray for a permanent peace.

Your children can participate in the observance of Memorial Day by accompanying you when you decorate graves and other memorials with flowers. You can use this time to discuss with your children why you are grateful to those who have died in battle, and why it is important for the world to be at peace.

Your family can hang its American Flag out on this day. This is also a good time of year to encourage your children to write a letter to the President of the United States. In it, they can write about why a peaceful world is important. Your children can also use this day to write thank-you notes to grandfathers, grandmothers, uncles, aunts, and other relatives who have served in the armed forces.

68. Flag Day

On June 14, 1777, John Adams introduced a proclamation to the Continental Congress which read, "Resolved, That the flag of the thirteen United States shall be thirteen stripes, alternate red and white; that the union be thirteen stars, white on a blue field, representing a new constellation."

Since then, Flag Day has been celebrated in the United States each year on June 14. Your children will like celebrating this holiday each year, too. It will help instill in them a sense of patriotism and a love for the flag.

You may wish to dress the family up in red, white and blue on this day. Your children will enjoy learning from you the proper way to hang the American flag. When they are older, they can take turns hanging it outside by themselves. Miniature, paper flags can be placed atop cupcakes, and can be used to decorate bowls of strawberry and vanilla ice cream, garnished with blueberries. Think red, white and blue . . . and let your imaginations go!

69. Father's Day

Father's Day originated in 1910 as the result of an idea set forth by Mrs. John B. Dodd of Spokane, Washington. President Calvin Coolidge lent his support to the idea in 1924, but it wasn't until 1972 that Father's Day became officially recognized by Public Law 92-278. Luckily, your children won't have to miss a single year of honoring Dear Ol' Dad.

Since Father's Day falls on the third Sunday in June, it is an ideal time of year to take Dad out for a day in the park. A Father's Day Picnic can feature all of Dad's favorite foods, which the children can help prepare. If Dad likes softball, a family game can be played. If you are short on players, you might want to invite other families from your neighborhood to participate in the Father's Day Picnic. Remember, too, that dads love to throw Frisbees, so have a few of those on hand, too.

You can top off the picnic each year by giving Dad a gift or two that he will really like, such as an easy chair, a bathrobe, or a new tennis racquet.

70. Independence Day

Children love the excitement of watching fireworks on the Fourth of July. So do parents! Therefore, Independence Day is a day that the whole family can look forward to, enjoy, and remember for many years to come.

You may wish to start off the day by explaining to your children that we celebrate the Fourth of July because it was on that day in 1776 that the Declaration of Independence was signed. Afterwards, your children, and others in the neighborhood, might enjoy decorating their bikes and wagons in red, white and blue, and having a parade through the neighborhood.

That evening, the whole family can watch fireworks together. Check your local newspaper for information about fireworks displays. There should be many impressive fireworks shows within driving distance. And, for extra fun, bring along several boxes of sparklers. You may wish to save a box or two of sparklers, as they make great additions to your children's birthday cakes later in the year!

SEPT 5 - Monday
LABOR DAY
Relax!

SEPT. 6 - Tuesday
Dr. Smith 10:20
Lunch with Jill - 12:30
shopping - 2:30
pick up laundry 4:15

71. Labor Day

Labor Day is celebrated on the first Monday in September. It became a federal holiday in 1894 when President Grover Cleveland put into law an act making it so.

Most parents will have Labor Day off from work. Since parents don't have to work on this day, and children don't have school on this day, it only makes sense that all family members be given the day off from any type of "labor." Mow the lawn next weekend, pull the weeds tomorrow, and wash the car on Saturday. This is a day for total devotion to relaxation!

Labor Day is a great day to treat the family to a movie. This should be a day of no work, and a whole lot of fun, for everyone. If you have an ice rink in town, your family might enjoy spending a portion of this warm day doing Figure 8's. Labor Day is also a great day for a barbecue in the backyard. Throughout the day, remember to relax and enjoy! This is what will make this a day for children to look forward to each year.

72. Grandparents Day

Grandparents Day falls on the first Sunday in September after Labor Day. It's a holiday which children can look forward to celebrating each year, even if their grandparents are no longer living.

Throughout the year, have double prints made when developing pictures of the family. The originals will go into the family album, and the doubles can be given to your children for their own albums and for their grandparents' albums. A photo album of children and grandchildren makes an ideal gift to grandparents on Grandparents Day. It is a gift that will be treasured and appreciated. This gift can be presented each year at a special family dinner given in honor of your children's grandparents.

If your children's grandparents are deceased, children can still honor them by looking through old family albums with you, listening to happy stories you tell your children about their grandparents' lives, and making a toast to their grandparents at a special family dinner that evening.

77. Hanukkah

On this, the Feast of Lights, families commemorate the victory of the Maccabees. The menorah is the symbol of this holiday. It has nine candles. One candle is the shamas, or lighting candle. The other eight candles represent the great miracle which occurred when the Eternal Light burned in the temple for eight days and nights on only one day's supply of oil.

The playing of games has long been associated with Hanukkah. The most popular is the game of dreidel. A dreidel is a four-sided top with letters representing "A great miracle happened there."

Children will enjoy singing the songs of Hanukkah with you. They will also enjoy decorating your home for the holiday with many traditional symbols, including the menorah and the ark, which was built to hold the Torah. The ark can hold five small Torahs, which the family can make out of construction paper. These serve to symbolize the five Books of Moses.

78. Christmas

On December 25, Christians throughout the world celebrate the birth of Jesus. Your family may wish to spend Christmas Eve attending a traditional midnight Christmas mass. Or, you might read "T'was the Night Before Christmas" to your children. Have your little ones set out a plate of cookies, milk and a letter for Santa (who writes back) before bed.

The Christmas celebration in your home might include many traditions which your children will long remember. You might begin by having your family cut down its own Christmas tree, provided, of course, that you live in a part of the country where this is possible! Wherever you get your tree, your children will love to help decorate it. Each year, you may wish to add a special Christmas ornament on which the year appears. These special, dated ornaments will help bring back memories of Christmasses past. And, don't forget the Christmas lights, Christmas cookies, Christmas caroling, and the mistletoe, all guaranteed to warm children's hearts.

79. New Year's Eve

New Year's Eve is a great time to share a wonderful holiday with your children without having to get on the highways.

Invite the neighbors over for a family style New Year's Eve party each year. Children will get a real kick out of decorating the house with streamers and balloons. Be sure to get plenty of noisemakers for the party, too! And, don't forget to take naps that afternoon!

Your children can help make an ice cream punch and lots of delicious goodies to munch on. Your New Year's Eve party is a perfect time for children to play with the board games and toys they received for Christmas or Hanukkah. But the best part of the party, for your children anyway, will be that they get to stay up past midnight! Have plenty of confetti ready for the children and parents to throw in the air at the stroke of midnight. Then, at precisely 12:00 a.m., give each of your children a big kiss, and wish them a Happy New Year!

Chapter Four: School Days

Besides the family, school is the most important institution in helping children develop into responsible, educated adults. And while our schools are given the responsibility for educating our children, it is important for parents to enhance and supplement a school's curriculum in a way that benefits the child's social and institutional education.

Suggestions made in this chapter are intended to instill a sense of the importance of education within the child. Additionally, there are activities to help a child develop pride and competence in school. Other ideas promote outside activities, such as sports, scouting and chores, which help a child learn about such things as competition, cooperation and responsibility.

School is serious business, and every child should be encouraged to do his or her very best. School should be promoted as a privilege and not a necessary evil. Allow and encourage your child to have fun when appropriate. But always expect full effort, too.

A family tradition of educational excellence is one of the best gifts you can give your child. It will last a lifetime, and it will be the most important asset your child has when he or she eventually leaves home.

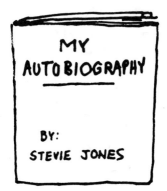

80. Yearly Autobiographies

Many stationery stores sell "School Days" books which are divided up by yearly grades. As such, there is a section in the book for "First Grade" entries, a section for "Second Grade" entries, and so on. These can be an invaluable record of your children's days in school. There are places for you to affix school pictures, enter immunization data, and write about your children's progress in school. In addition, these books usually contain pouches, in which you can place your children's report cards and other pertinent written material.

You can also encourage your children to write yearly autobiographies which can be stored in the "School Days" pouches. These essays should be written in your children's own handwriting. You might encourage your children to write about their year in school, their favorite subjects, their favorite friends and their teachers. As the children get older, you can encourage them to write about their goals in life. When your children are all grown up, they will enjoy reminiscing about their school days.

81. "Showing Off" Bulletin Board

From time to time, each of your children will bring home something from school that they and you will be really proud of. Whenever possible, these items (such as report cards or term papers) can be placed on your "Showing Off" Bulletin Board, which can be made out of cork.

This should be a separate board from that which the family tacks phone messages on! This board is designed solely to display outstanding work by your children. And, it's important to balance the number of items each child has on the "Showing Off" bulletin board, so that all of your children are equally represented on the board.

You may wish to add stickers (in the shapes of stars, hearts, exclamation points, arrows) to your children's works. Or you can add your own written comments, such as "Way to Go!," "Nice Work!," or "Wowie Zowie!" The idea is to encourage your children to take pride in a job well done. The attention you pay to their hard work will long be remembered.

82. Trip to the Library

Parents wishing to give their children an extra advantage in school might consider taking the whole family to the library every Saturday morning. Your children will look forward to these outings in no time!

Trips to the library need to be part of your weekly routine in order to make a difference in the lives of your children. If your children show a particular interest in something, you can help them find new library books about that topic. Or, if they are studying something interesting in school, you might point out a few relevant books which they might enjoy.

Parents, too, should use the Saturday morning visits to the library to check out books. This not only sets a good example for the children, but can bring great reading pleasure to you as well. Remember, with the proliferation of electronic media, you will need to go out of your way to help your children get back to the basics of reading. Well-read children grow up to be well-read, and often, very successful, adults.

83. First Day in Kindergarten

The first day in kindergarten (or First Grade, if your school has no kindergarten), can be the scariest day of all. But, if you treat this day as something very special, your children will grow up remembering this day with great fondness.

During the months preceding the first day of kindergarten, you can talk to your children about how wonderful, and grown-up, school is. You can hang a calendar in your little ones' bedrooms, so they can help you mark off the days until they will get to go to school for the very first time.

When the first day of kindergarten finally arrives, you can dress your children up in their "Sunday best." Be sure to take a picture of your children on this important day. You might want to accompany your children right to their classrooms on this special day. After school, you may wish to tape record your children as they tell you about their first days in school. They'll get a kick out of listening to this tape in years to come.

84. Little League

Whether your children choose to participate in Little League or girls' softball, or soccer, or any other after-school sports, you can help make these activities even more memorable for them.

Your children might really enjoy having the family at their games to cheer them on. If this is the case, you might choose to make it a tradition to take the family out for pizza or hamburgers after each game, whether the team wins or loses. Children will look back on these days with great fondness if you give them lots of encouragement and support, no matter what kind of athletes they are.

Be sure to get a team photo which can be added to the family scrapbook. In addition, you may wish to have team photos enlarged and framed for hanging in your children's bedrooms. If your children win trophies or ribbons for their efforts, you can help build a special shelf in their rooms to display their awards.

85. Girl Scouts/Boy Scouts

Scouting is good, clean, memorable fun for both boys and girls. This is an activity that parents can participate in actively with their children, either as troop leaders or as sideline cheerleaders.

Whether your children participate in Brownies, Cub Scouts, Indian Guides, 4-H, Future Farmers of America, Camp Fire Girls, Girl Scouts, Boy Scouts, or any other such organization, they will likely get involved with many outside projects. You can help your children remember these times by encouraging them to make related entries into the family journal, and by taking pictures of special events. Be sure to get a picture of your children's troops or clubs, and include these in the family album.

If your children earn badges or other awards, these can be sewn directly to their uniforms. Later, when your children no longer participate in these organizations, you can add badges and awards to the family scrapbook where they won't get lost.

86. Good Report Cards

Parents can help shape their children's academic future by always making a big fuss about good report cards. Your children will look back with great fondness on the days in which you bent over backwards to show them how proud you were of them, and the work they were doing in school.

You may wish to reward good report cards with money. You may wish to reward them by allowing your children to be excused from household chores for a week. In any case, good report cards look just great on the refrigerator where everyone can see them.

Keep in mind that good report cards don't necessarily mean report cards with straight A's. If you feel that your children are doing their absolute best in school, then their grades should be considered "good," and rewarded as such. You can make your children feel exceedingly good about school and themselves by celebrating their good grades with special dinners or gifts. Remember, children who are told they are bright usually grow up bright.

87. Sack Lunches

Sack lunches, believe it or not, can be the source of many fond childhood memories.

When your children are in elementary school, they will enjoy all of the colorful drawings you add to the outside of their sack lunches. And, children of all ages will enjoy that one special day of the week, each week, when you prepare their favorite lunches. They'll look forward to "Friday" lunches, for example, with eager anticipation.

As your children grow older, you can include secret messages inside their sack lunches. You may wish to include some of your children's favorite comic strips. Or, you may wish to include a puzzle or two to keep them occupied through lunch. Every so often, such as on exam days, you might slip a note inside their sack lunches telling them that a special surprise awaits them after school. When they get home, you can treat them to hot chocolate chip cookies or an afternoon of horseback riding.

88. Sick Days

Days during which your children are home sick from school can be the worst days while they are living them, and among the best days when they are remembering them.

As Mary Poppins would say, "A spoonful of sugar helps the medicine go down." The point is that you can help make sick days turn into special days by giving your sick children little treats that will make them feel better, such as ice cream, coloring books, or stuffed animals. To keep your sick children comfortable, you may wish to lay them on the couch in front of the TV, where they will stay still, and probably fall asleep. When it comes to getting fluids down them, you might like to try special, brightly colored cups and snazzy straws, both of which hold great appeal for children.

And, for goodness sake, remember the chicken soup! Children, for some reason, grow up remembering how their parents helped bring them back to health with this wonderful remedy. It's all part of growing up!

89. Foul Weather Days

What in the world can kids do on rainy days that they will remember long into adulthood?

With a little help from you, they can have the time of their lives! Simply dress the kids up in rain slickers, rain boots, rain hats and umbrellas, and let them jump up and down in the rain puddles outside! If you bundle them up properly, they won't catch cold, and they will have lots and lots of fun. Afterwards, bring them inside for hot tomato soup and sandwiches. After lunch, sit them in front of the fireplace for a cozy game of Clue, Life, or Yahtzee. When the rain stops and the sun begins to shine again, take the kids out in search of the rainbow and the pot of gold!

And remember that younger children will delight in hearing you read "The Cat in the Hat," perhaps the most wonderful rainy day book ever written for children. Feel free to read this book every time it rains, as children never tire of this story.

90. Inviting Teacher to Dinner

At the end of the school year, after grades are in, and classes are out, you may wish to ask your children if they would like to invite their favorite teachers over for dinner. This serves as a very nice and personal way of thanking teachers who have been particularly influential in the lives of your children.

After dinner, your children can present their teachers with a special gift, such as a basket of flowers, a hand-knitted scarf, or a thank-you poem. You will be amazed at how much your children will look forward to such an occasion, and how much they will treasure the memories long into the future.

In this same regard, you can also help your children express their appreciation to their teachers during the school year by helping them make Valentine's Day cards for their teachers, and by helping them bake cookies for their teachers at Christmas.

91. After-School Snacks

Let's face it. Sometimes the best part of school is hearing the last bell of the day. To many children, that signifies the end of drudgery and the beginning of snacktime!

Your children may be among those who truly look forward to their after-school snacks each day. The trick to making these snacks really special is to insist that your children sit down at the table for them, instead of grabbing the snacks and running outside with them!

What types of things make memorable snacks? Kool-Aid and anything hot out of the oven. It's that simple. You may wish to try hot bread sticks, or hot oatmeal cookies, or hot nachos, or hot blueberry muffins. Your children will long remember what it was like to come home from a long day at school and be met at the door by the aroma of something delicious coming from the oven. Is the quickest way to a child's heart through his or her stomach? You better believe it is! Especially after school!

92. Babysitters

Leaving your children with a babysitter can be somewhat traumatic for the kids, or it can be a time that your children will actually look forward to. The key is to make the time spent with a babysitter extra special.

The easiest way to get your children to look forward to having a babysitter is to extend their bedtimes by a half hour or an hour on that night. Any time kids get to stay up late, they're going to be excited. Next, you might designate "babysitter night" as "chocolate sundae" night. Kids will delight in building their own sundaes with the babysitter. Go all out, too! Leave ice cream, whipped cream, nuts, fudge topping and cherries for the babysitter. Of course, a very nutritious dinner should be eaten first!

And, in order to make those nights on which the babysitter spends with your children really special, encourage the babysitter and your children to play board games or word games, or to put together puzzles, instead of spending the evening watching television.

93. Homework

How can parents make homework something which children will look forward to, and recall with some fondness when they become adults? There are a few tricks you might want to consider.

Start off by providing all of your children with desks of their own. This is an investment which will reap great rewards. You and your children can pick out, together, such items as desk lamps, blotters, pencil holders and other homework supplies. Children who take great pride in their desks will take great pride in their homework.

Next, you might wish to monitor your children's homework carefully. You can make sure that they do it before they watch TV. When they have done what you consider to be a good job on their homework, let them know. A little praise will go a long way! Then, when your children bring home graded homework which their teachers liked, be sure to post the homework on your children's bulletin boards. Add your own star stickers, too!

welcome to
CAMP
WINAMUNGA

94. Summer Vacation

Summer vacation is a great time for children to participate in activities that they don't have time for during the school year.

Younger children might enjoy spending the summer learning how to ride horses. They may also enjoy beginning, intermediate and advanced swimming classes. If your town happens to put on a parade in the summer, your children will no doubt enjoy working on one of the floats.

Older children might enjoy spending the summer getting in shape. Your family may wish to invest in some exercise equipment. And summer mornings are ideal for a family to jog around the neighborhood before breakfast. Evenings are great for family bike rides around town.

In addition, children of all ages will enjoy going to summer camp. Simply pick the camp that features the kinds of activities your children love, and they will have the time of their lives.

95. Chores

As long as "chore time" isn't "bore time," your children will look back on this part of their lives with at least a bit of fondness!

If you have children who leave their dirty laundry all over their closets, instead of putting it in the laundry basket, try this trick. Buy each of your children his or her own laundry basket. Install a "Nerf" basketball hoop above the laundry baskets in their closets. Then, watch as your children shoot baskets with their dirty clothes, resulting in clean floors and filled baskets. And, as soon as your children are old enough to operate a washer and dryer, insist that they do their own laundry.

For other chores around the house, you can help your children look forward to them by giving each child a small, personal AM/FM radio with headphones. You will be surprised at how well your children will do their chores if they can "whistle while they work!" And, if you wish, a weekly allowance can be given for a job well done.

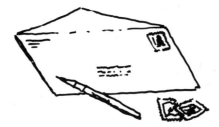

96. Pen Pals

Pen pals give your children something to look forward to. Whether these pen pals are friends who have moved out of town, or friends they have never met from overseas, your children will enjoy and long remember writing and receiving letters.

You may, as a family, choose to "adopt" an overseas foster child. Many social service agencies can help you link up with a child overseas who can use your help. The small donation you make each month is used to help feed, clothe, educate and care for the child. And your children can correspond with the child through an interpreter, if necessary. It's an educational and heart-warming experience for your children and the child overseas.

In addition, your children will enjoy being pen pals with friends who have moved out of town. If possible, arrange for your children to visit their friends on a family vacation. And be sure to save all their letters.

97. School Plays

From time to time, your children will have the opportunity in school to take center stage. This is a most exciting time in their lives, and you can help them remember these moments in several ways.

You may wish to check with your children's teachers to see if it would be all right to videotape their school plays. Nowadays, video camcorders are so small and lightweight, that they can be set up easily in the audience. Most camcorders will give you very good audio and video signals. These videotapes will bring lots of pleasure and laughter in years to come.

In addition, you may wish to take special photographs of the casts after the performances. If possible, include the teachers in these snapshots. After the photographs have been developed, you can add them to the family scrapbook, along with copies of your children's scripts. Be sure to highlight your children's lines in the plays. Playbills, if handed out at the school plays, can also be included in the family scrapbook.

98. Family Safety

There aren't too many things which you will teach your children in life that are more important than rules about family safety. These rules should be taught with the utmost in care and perseverance. Taught properly, these rules will stick with your children throughout their lives.

Poison stickers, obtained from your local Poison Control office or local pharmacy, should be placed on everything in the house that you want little children to stay away from. Young children should also be taught their address and phone number, how to safely cross the street, how to react around strangers, where to go in an emergency, and how to dial "911."

Family fire drills should also be held every few months. Children should be taught what to do in the event of a fire, and how to check if the smoke detectors are working properly. Also, teach everyone in the family to wear seat belts. And, as your kids grow older, you can enroll the whole family in a CPR class. These are all lessons in life that will last forever.

99. First Date

First dates are a time of severe jitters . . . for your children and for you! But, if you think *you're* nervous, multiply that feeling by ten, and it will give you an idea of how nervous your children are.

No matter what you do, your children will probably always remember their first dates. But you can encourage them to remember this milestone by having them write in their diaries before and after their first dates. And, if your children will allow you to do so, take a picture of them when their dates come to pick them up. If you have sons, you may be out of luck! But, perhaps their dates' mothers can take a picture for you.

A first date is also a wonderful occasion to buy your children a special outfit. Go ahead and splurge, because this is a once-in-a-lifetime event. And what first date would be complete without a curfew? Your children probably won't like it, but they are certain to remember it, and pass it on.

```
┌─────────────────────────────┐
│  THIS BOOK BELONGS           │
│         TO:                  │
│   Jimmy Smith                │
│  DATE: 5/8/87                │
└─────────────────────────────┘
```

100. Personal Libraries

Teaching your children to have a love for books is easy if you set a good example for them. Earlier in this book, you may have noticed a section about taking your family to the library on a weekly basis. That's one way to help them develop an interest in books. Here's another.

You may wish to enroll your family in a book club. Regular book purchases can be made for family books. Then, as you earn book dividends, children can use them to pick out books of their very own.

In order to personalize these books, give each of your children special bookplates which they can affix to their own books. And, remember, jazzy bookmarks make great stocking stuffers at Christmas.

Then find a place in each of your children's rooms for a bookshelf or bookcase. In order to start off their collections, you may wish to give each of your children their own dictionaries and thesauruses.

101. High School Annuals/Portraits

A high school annual makes an excellent gift from parents to their children. And high school portraits should be included with all graduation announcements.

Your children's high school annuals will be among the items they will look at and treasure for the rest of their lives. But you may wish to suggest that you keep their annuals at home for safe keeping when your children go away to college. High school annuals really have a knack for getting lost, due to all the moves children make during their college years.

High school portraits (usually those featured in high school annuals) are available for purchase at most high schools. These make excellent gifts to adoring grandparents, uncles and aunts. Be sure to order plenty of the wallet-sized portraits, as your high school seniors will probably want to exchange these pictures with their friends. Autographed pictures of friends make very memorable additions to your children's scrapbooks.

102. High School Graduation

Your children's high school graduations will be a time of great joy and celebration for your family. Savor these moments, as they are very special once-in-a-lifetime events.

You may wish to buy a new dress or a new suit for each of your graduating seniors. They'll want to look their best on this day. And high school graduations are an excellent time for you to give your children an engraved watch which they can treasure in the years ahead.

Your family can also treat your graduating seniors to a night on the town, featuring dinner and a live show. At dinner, you can start a family tradition of offering a toast to your graduates, and having a special cake delivered to your table. And after the day is through, and the excitement has died down, you can have your high school seniors' diplomas framed. Framed diplomas can be displayed in the family library or in your children's bedrooms.

103. Prom Night

Prom Night should be a night of magical dreams come true for your children. It's a night of elegance, sparkle and excitement. And parents can help make Prom Night a night to remember.

If you have a sewing machine and a daughter, you might want to consider making her prom dress. Your daughter will enjoy shopping with you for the material and the pattern. Beautiful dresses can be made from silk, satin, taffeta or chiffon. If you have a son, he will enjoy having you accompany him to the tuxedo rental store. And wait until you see your children all dressed up in their prom clothes! You won't believe your eyes!

Prom pictures will be taken at the dance, and if you wish, you can surprise your children by buying the pictures for them. Also, be sure to take pictures of your children with their dates before they leave for the dance. These pictures look wonderful in sterling silver frames. They are a keepsake which can be beautifully displayed in the family library.

107. Meals for the Homeless

Once a year, you can have a family tradition of preparing meals for the homeless. City or state homeless agencies can give you more information about how you can help. You may even check with your local church, since many of them also get actively involved in providing needed assistance.

As your children work alongside you in an effort to help feed the homeless, they will learn a great deal about those less fortunate than they, and it will help them learn to appreciate their own family life more.

Some agencies prefer that families help out the homeless by collecting and delivering canned foods to various shelters around town. If this is the case in your community, your family can call upon neighbors to donate canned foods to local shelters. Your children can go door-to-door with you, pulling a wagon, with the goal of filling it with food to feed the hungry. Humanitarian gestures on the part of your children will help them feel good about themselves and compassionate towards the needy.

108. Finger Food Night

This is one night your children are bound to love, and ask for again and again.

Finger Food Night is a night during which all dinner items are eaten without the benefit of silverware. No forks, no knives, no spoons! For children who love to play with their food, this is a dream come true.

For the main dish, you might serve pizza, chicken strips, spareribs, fried shrimp, tacos, or beef kabobs. Fruits might include grapes, raisins, apples, pears, bananas or watermelon. Vegetables might include carrot sticks, celery sticks, tater tots, or corn on the cob. For dessert, you might consider popsicles, ice cream cones, cookies, or popcorn.

And since there won't be any silverware to wash, you may want to serve the meal using paper plates, paper cups and paper place mats. It'll be a snap to clean up afterwards!

109. Candlelight Dinners

During the winter, when the days are short and the nights are long, your family can warm the chill in the air by occasionally serving candlelight dinners.

Candlelight dinners are particularly appropriate on special occasions, such as birthdays, anniversaries, the first day of winter, and the first day each year when it snows.

Children should be instructed to dress up for dinner. You can use your good silverware, tablecloths, cloth napkins and china for these dinners. Special instruction in proper etiquette can also be given at this time.

Candlelight dinners are ideal times to serve roast beef, turkey, or steak. Wine glasses may be filled with sparkling cider for the children and wine for the adults. Your children will feel very grown up at these dinners, and will look forward to dining again in this fashion.

110. Sunday Brunch

In this world of instant coffee, Instant Breakfast, and Egg McMuffins, it's nice to know that families can set aside one morning a week for a truly scrumptious and balanced meal.

Your children will really look forward to Sunday brunch each week. Some Sundays you may choose to have brunch out at a restaurant, and some Sundays you may choose to have brunch at home. Either way, your children will appreciate the festive nature of Sunday brunch, and every so often, they may even go to bed Saturday dreaming about it!

If you serve Sunday brunch at home, your children can pitch in by helping you make the blueberry muffins, the waffles or the orange juice. Be sure to have lots of fresh fruit on hand, as children really seem to favor it at Sunday brunch. And in order to make Sunday brunch really memorable, the whole family should sit down together for this meal, rather than grab it on the run. Can't you almost smell that sausage sizzling?

111. Neighborhood Progressive Dinners

Here's a truly fun way to treat your children to dinner! Team up with your favorite neighbors and have a neighborhood progressive dinner.

These dinners are amazingly simple to prepare. The first family prepares the appetizer. The second family prepares the main course. And the third family prepares the dessert.

All three families meet at the first family's home to eat the appetizer. Then all three families go to the second family's home for the main course. Finally, all three families visit the third family's home for the dessert. This is a lot of fun for children because it's such a change of pace. It fills an evening a whole lot better than TV ever could!

Neighborhood progressive dinners are especially memorable when they have a theme to them. Perhaps you and your neighbors might try an Italian or Mexican progressive dinner. It's an experience your kids won't forget!

112. Dinner with Great Americans

Have you or your children ever wished you could have Abraham Lincoln over for dinner? Or perhaps George Washington or Betsy Ross? It's possible, you know, to have any number of great Americans over for dinner. All you need is a little spirit and a whole lot of imagination!

This is a good dinner to plan over spring vacation. Have each member of your family choose a famous American and dress up as this person for your "Dinner with Great Americans." Mom might dress up as Martha Washington, and Dad might dress up as her husband, George. Your children might dress up as Benjamin Franklin, Abraham Lincoln, Betsy Ross or Albert Einstein. During dinner, have everyone act as if he or she is indeed one of these famous people. Your family is bound to come up with some fascinating table talk! Remember, don't slip out of character!

Spring vacation can be spent making costumes for this dinner. This will be a great dinner to capture with your videocassette recorder!

113. Upside Down Day

Upside Down Day is a day on which dinner is served first thing in the morning, breakfast is served at night, and midnight snacks are served at noon.

This will delight the youngest members of your family and even your older children will enjoy having things shaken up a bit!

For breakfast, you can serve steak, baked potatoes, salad and pineapple upside down cake. At noon, try serving celery stuffed with peanut butter and strawberry sherbert. At dinner time, you can serve scrambled eggs, apple juice and toast.

What's the best day of the year to celebrate Upside Down Day? Why, April 1, of course. Granted, this is a goofy day, but your children will look back on this celebration with great fondness. And the topper of the day might be a picture you take of your family standing on their heads!

114. Talent Show Dinner

Your children can prepare all year long for your annual Family Talent Show Dinner. At this feast, each member of the family is assigned the task of preparing his or her most spectacular edible masterpiece.

Dinner course assignments can change on a yearly basis, so one year Mom might make the main course, Dad might make the appetizer, your son might make the vegetables, and your daughter might make the dessert. The following year, Mom would make the appetizer, Dad would make the vegetables, your son would make the dessert, and your daughter would make the main course. And so on.

After showing off your culinary delights, you can put on a real live family talent show, in which you can show off your other talents. It will be lots of fun to use this occasion to offer tumultuous applause and praise to each family member. This will be another event which makes great family viewing in years to come, so be sure to use your camcorder.

115. TV Dinners

On TV Dinner Night at your home, all members of your family can dress up as their favorite TV stars.

For example, you may wish to have a "Magnum P.I." TV Dinner Night. This should be held on the same night of the week as the program airs. Everyone in the family can dress in Hawaiian attire. You can really add to the enjoyment of TV Dinner Night by throwing a luau in your backyard. Care to go all out? Rent a red Ferrari for the night, and take the family out for macadamia nut ice cream after dinner.

Other TV shows which lend themselves nicely to TV Dinner Night include Dynasty (wear lots of rhinestones and serve caviar), Dallas (throw a real Texas barbecue in your backyard), and Newhart (serve dinner country style, and have the kids dress up as Larry, Darryl and Darryl). TV Dinner Night is a wacky idea, but kids will love and remember it!

116. Cinco de Mayo Dinner

On May 5th each year, your family can have fun with food by preparing a Cinco de Mayo Mexican dinner. This will be particularly enjoyable for your children if they have learned to speak a bit of Spanish. You can also help your children dress up in colorful costumes for this very special feast.

Your children can be a great help to you when you are preparing the meal. Kids especially enjoy mashing the avocados to make guacamole dip. They can also help out making the nachos, since these are very simple to prepare. Tacos, enchiladas, burritos, chimichangas, tortillas, and ensaladas are all easy to prepare, and you will find recipes for these in many popular cookbooks.

Many import stores carry pinatas, and if you can find one, your children will enjoy cracking it open to get to the candies inside. Pinatas can be suspended from a tree in your backyard. A wonderful time will be had by all, and you'll be hearing your children say, "Muchas, muchas gracias."

117. Seasonal Meal Flip-Flops

Whoever heard of Thanksgiving in July? Or summer in January? Your children, of course, providing they have been raised in a household serving Seasonal Meal Flip-Flops!

If you are a family with an outdoor barbecue, you may get to the point by the end of July when you can no longer face another hamburger for dinner. Well, here comes Seasonal Meal Flip-Flops to the rescue. Try surprising your children this summer with a full Thanksgiving meal, trimmings and all. This will be such a special, and unexpected pleasure, that they are bound to ask for it every summer!

And, during the middle of winter, when your children have had it with hot soup, hot stew, and hot chocolate, how about throwing a real picnic right on your own family room floor? Throw down a picnic blanket, set out paper plates, plastic cups, silverware, and napkins, and you're ready! Kids will welcome the sight of lemonade, fried chicken and potato salad!

118. My Favorite Meal

Your children will probably pass this family tradition down to their children someday, since it's a tradition that is both fun and tasty!

Let's say your daughter was born on January 15th. As soon as she starts eating solid foods, and until she moves out of the house when she is a young adult, your family can designate the 15th of every month as her Favorite Meal Day. On that day, serve her favorite foods, whether they be salmon, spaghetti, sandwiches or sushi. She gets to decide the fare for any one meal that day. That's twelve "guaranteed delicious" meals a year!

Likewise, if your son was born on May 19th, your family can serve his favorite foods on the 19th of each month, every month. Do the same for Mom, Dad, and all the children. And if you have two birthdays which fall on the same day of the month, simply have one person choose the lunch menu and one person choose the dinner menu. This is also an ideal time to teach your children how to prepare their favorite meals, too!

119. Family Nationality Meals

Chances are both of your children's parents are from an interesting mix of nationalities. You may be Irish, Scottish and English, and your spouse may be Austrian, German and French. Whatever your nationality, your children will get a kick out of celebrating your "roots" with Family Nationality Meals."

These make nice Saturday night dinners since their preparation time is usually a bit longer than your typical family meals. If you are Irish, for example, you may wish to prepare corned beef or Irish Stew. If your spouse is Italian, you may wish to prepare fettucini or authentic Italian spaghetti.

You can involve your children in "Family Nationality Meals" by giving them some ethnic cookbooks, and letting them decide which meals they would like to try. Playing some ethnic music on your stereo while you are cooking will really put you and your children in the mood for these dinners!

120. Kids-in-Charge Meals

As your children grow older, you may want to let them in on some of the fun involved with cooking by designating a certain day each week for "Kids-in-Charge" meals.

The trick to making these meals a smashing success is for parents to stay completely out of the kitchen while the children are preparing the meals. Naturally, this will require that you have spent many previous days (or years) teaching them how to cook.

Children can do everything for these meals. They can plan the meals, pick out the ingredients at the store, prepare the meals, serve the meals, and clean up after the meals. You may be surprised at the interest your children take in these special meals. Don't be surprised if they really go all out, with gourmet main dishes, candlelight, and sumptuous desserts.

Children and parents will remember these feasts with great fondness!

121. Murder Mystery Dinners

On very special occasions each year, your family can enjoy a murder mystery dinner, complete with fine foods, suspects, and clues, and culminating in the solving of a murder mystery. It's all done in fun, of course, but your children will find the evening deliciously scary!

Most large toy and some specialty stores carry box games which you can use for these dinners. One example is "How to Host a Murder." These games come complete with an audio cassette tape which reveals details of the murder, a blueprint of the scene of the crime, a host guide, instructions, eight guest invitations, eight top-secret clue manuals, sealed clues, name tags, costume suggestions, and dinner menus.

Invite guests to participate in this Murder Mystery Dinner so that you have eight people all together, including yourselves and your children. Dinner is worked into the evening as participants sift through clues. These evenings amount to four hours of exceptionally good food and great fun!

122. Hello Hollywood Night

Each year, on the night of the Academy Awards presentations, your family can share in the glamour of the evening by celebrating "Hello Hollywood Night."

This is a great opportunity to have your friends and your children's friends over for dinner. Let everyone know that this is strictly a "dress up night." Boas, bangles, rhinestones, wild hairdos, fake furs, bow ties, silver gloves, sunglasses, and anything else that will make you look glamorous is appropriate for this evening at the Oscars!

Dinner should be served around the television set, so the whole family and any invited friends can watch the Academy Awards. If you really want to go all out, you may even hire someone to cater this affair! Serve such spectacular dishes as prime rib and flaming desserts to really "wow" the family. And be sure to take plenty of pictures of your "family stars." Naturally, these should be "autographed" and put into the family album!

123. Grammy Night

Like "Hello Hollywood Night," "Grammy Night" is a night planned around the TV set. Instead of dressing up in your glamorous best, this is a night for dressing up as your favorite rock star and celebrating with a dinner fit for a great rock concert.

Parents will really feel the generation gap on this evening! But don't worry! It'll all be in good fun! Parents can dress up as the Beatles, the Rolling Stones, the Grateful Dead, the Monkees, or the Supremes. Your kids can dress up as the Police, Michael Jackson, Bruce Springsteen, or Madonna (good grief!). Invite your children's friends and neighbors to participate, too. But remember to ask everyone to dress up as a rock star.

Serve "teen food" on "Grammy Night." Try hot dogs, french fries and homemade chocolate milkshakes. Serve dinner buffet style, around the coffee table, in front of the television. This will be a yearly event your children will really look forward to!

124. Japanese Dinner

Children of all ages will look forward to having Japanese dinners at home. Parents, too, will enjoy these special occasion meals as they are quiet, relaxing, and very conducive to family conversation.

Start off with a good Japanese cookbook. Pick dishes that your children will enjoy, but just in case they don't, be sure to make plenty of rice!

Dinner can be served "Japanese style," around a low coffee table. The family can sit on pillows around the table. Your children will enjoy eating the meal with chopsticks after you have given them lessons. If the lessons don't work, don't worry! The children can always use forks!

In the background, play soft, soothing Japanese music. Your family might also enjoy wearing kimonos, socks and thongs. Kimonos are simple to sew, and making one for each family member might be an excellent family project.

125. "Did You Know That . . ."

Holiday meals and family reunion meals are a wonderful occasion to use the "Did You Know That" technique at the dinner table. This is an activity that will pique your children's interest about the lives of other family members.

Here's an example of how to plan for this event. Arrange ahead of time with a relative who will be at the meal to participate in this. Let this relative know that towards the end of the meal, you will ask your children, "Did you know that Uncle Bill was a World War II flying ace?" Ask Uncle Bill to be ready to tell the story of his flying ace days with the kind of vivid detail your children will love.

After dinner, you might want to suggest to your children that they write either in the family diary or their personal diaries about Uncle Bill and his adventures. This will help keep the memories alive.

126. Table Talk

Here's a family custom that your children will look back upon with great fondness. It's a chance for some peaceful "Table Talk."

Once or twice a year, each parent should take each child out to dinner at a nice, quiet restaurant for a one-on-one meal. This will provide an excellent opportunity for you to understand your children better, and for your children to understand you better. Use this opportunity to enjoy each other's company in a nonauthoritative atmosphere, when you can relax and get to know another better.

Having "Table Talk" dinners with grandparents and grandchildren is also an excellent idea. Remember, the key is to have one grandparent and one grandchild together for this activity. It will make both people feel so special, and this activity is guaranteed to create strong and lasting memories.

Chapter Six:
Special Occasions

There are special times in the life of each child that will be remembered for years to come. Birthdays are the most obvious example. But other days and moments have importance to the child and the family as well. Wedding annivesaries, for example, celebrate love and commitment, and the formation of the family. They are a perfect example of a special occasion which can be celebrated by children and parents.

Other moments of the year can also be times to celebrate or reflect. An ancestor's birthday or the day he or she entered America might serve as a special time to take out the family tree and study it. Bedtime is an ideal time to discuss the day's events with a child, reinforce important lessons and reflect on good fortune.

These special occasions should be actively promoted by parents. Special talents can be toasted on the night of a recital or the opening of the school's science fair. Achievement of special rank in scouts should be honored by the whole family. Important family values and traditions should be remembered and incorporated into many special occasions. Fly the family flag. Bring out the family tablecloth. Make the occasion one to be remembered.

127. Family Time Capsule

Each year, during your New Year's Day dinner, you and your children can participate in a tradition which will surely become one of the most enjoyed traditions in your family: the opening of your family time capsule.

Your family time capsule can consist of simple shoe boxes, in which your family has placed memorabilia from years past. Items which you may include are videotapes of your family's favorite TV programs for the year, audio cassette recordings of your children's voices, contemporary outfits which your children have outgrown, family photographs, notes from teachers, newspaper stories, TIME magazine's "Man of the Year" issue, and audio cassettes of your family's favorite songs of the year. The shoe boxes should be tightly sealed, and labeled on the outside with the year.

Then during your New Year's Day dinner, the family can choose a box, perhaps from five or ten years ago, to open and enjoy. Later, a new box for the present year should be assembled and stored away.

128. The Cuddle Bear

There will inevitably be times in your children's lives when they will be heartbroken over unrequited love, or they will be sick in bed with the chicken pox, or they will strike out in the bottom of the ninth with the bases loaded. When the tears begin to flow, sometimes the only thing which might help is the family "Cuddle Bear."

The Cuddle Bear can be any old bear from any old toy store. The important thing is that the Cuddle Bear only show up at times when family members are really feeling sad. It should have a sweet face, and be very huggable. Just the sight of the family Cuddle Bear should bring smiles to even the saddest little faces.

Remember that parents, too, have sad days, and your children will want to bring you the Cuddle Bear on those occasions when you need cheering. Therefore, keep the Cuddle Bear in a place where everyone can get to it. It can serve as your family's "bearer" of good tidings during tough times.

129. Grandparents' Birthdays

Grandparents' birthdays can be a time of great joy for your children. During the course of the year, your children can help put together a photo album or photo montage which can be given to their grandparents on their birthdays. Your children can also help bake birthday cakes and put up party decorations. And they can help you choose and play birthday party music which was popular during their grandparents' teen years.

A short story about the grandparents which your children can write in their own words makes a lovely and memorable birthday gift. Let's say you have an eight-year-old daughter. She can spend some quiet time with Grandma on her birthday, asking her what life was like when she was eight. Your daughter can record this conversation on audiotape or videotape. Later, she can write a short essay based on her conversation, and give it to Grandma as a gift. This makes a great present for grandparents and provides an excellent way for children to better understand their family heritage.

130. Parents' Wedding Anniversary

If your children live in a two-parent family, they will get an enormous amount of pleasure out of seeing you renew your wedding vows on your tenth or twentieth wedding anniversary. If you are among the lucky ones who can still fit into your wedding clothes, go ahead and get all dressed up for the occasion. But even if you can't squeeze your size-14 body into your size-10 wedding dress, don't worry! You'll look just as great in any dress-up outfit you have in your closet.

If possible, renew your wedding vows in the place in which you and your spouse got married. If this site is far away, your family can plan a special vacation around traveling there.

Your children can serve as your attendants. It needn't be an event attended by anyone else but your family, if you wish. The important thing is to renew your vows under the most joyous circumstances, and to share with your children the special love you feel for each other and for them.

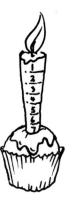

131. Children's Birthdays

Nothing quite lights up children's birthdays like the sight of their very own birthday candles, decorated with numbers, ranging from one to 21. These delightful birthday candles are available in department and specialty stores. You can light the candles each year on your children's birthdays, to allow the candles to burn down to your children's new ages.

Another tradition which your children will look forward to year after year is a birthday party with all the trimmings . . . cakes, ice cream, candles, balloons, party hats, streamers, party games and party favors. Even if you just have small family parties, birthdays are a time of great anticipation for children, and you can really bring smiles to their faces by throwing birthday parties for them every year until they are 18 years old! In addition, you may wish to give your children a very special gift each year, in addition to toys or clothes. A silver cup, Grandpa's pocket watch or a charm bracelet are each gifts which children will long treasure. You may wish to give your children special treasure chests in which to keep these mementos.

132. Birthday Recordings

Children grow up so quickly that it is sometimes hard to believe that they were ever small. But you can capture those innocent days of youth by making annual audio cassette recordings of your children's voices on their birthdays.

You may prefer to record your children's voices, along with the voices of their friends, at their birthday parties. Or, if you wish to obtain a more formal recording, take your child aside before or after the party and ask questions about his or her favorite things, such as favorite foods, favorite music, favorite friends, favorite TV shows, favorite activities and favorite subjects in school.

These birthday recordings can also be taken by using a video camera with audio capability. As with all treasured recordings, be certain to label the tapes with the date and other pertinent information, and store them upright in a cool environment.

133. Birthday Quilts

There is a very special moment in your children's lives — the day they reach the age of 21. On that day, many parents finally consider their children to be adults, although they have been able to vote since they were 18. There is a special gift that you can give to your children on their 21st birthdays which will commemorate this very special occasion.

It is a birthday quilt, which you can begin making as each of your children reach the age of one. The quilt can contain 20 panels which can be situated four panels across by five panels down. Each panel, which you can construct on each child's birthday, can depict something which that child really loved during that year of his or her life. For example, the one-year-old panel may have Winnie-the-Pooh on it, and the eight-year-old panel might have roller skates on it. Make panels for birthdays 1-20, and on the 21st birthday, sew the panels together to make a quilt. This makes a most meaningful and appreciated 21st birthday present.

134. Planned Birthday Gifts

Toys and clothes make wonderful birthday gifts for children, as do special planned birthday gifts, such as family heirlooms.

On your child's tenth or eleventh birthday, an older relative or grandparent can give your child an historical momento from your family's history. Perhaps this might be a family heirloom, such as Grandfather's pocket watch or Grandmother's gold locket. It is a good idea to talk about this gift for a year or two before the birthday on which it is given. That way, your child will have plenty of time to come to appreciate the importance of the gift.

When the gift is given on your child's birthday, be certain that the story relating to the gift's history is retold to your child. A special place might be found in your child's room for this heirloom. After receiving this gift, you can encourage your child to write in his or her personal diary about the gift and why it will be treasured.

135. Sharing Your Talents

Parents and grandparents possess many unique talents and skills which can be shared with children. Doing so will provide you with the opportunity to link your family's past with its present and its future.

Grandpa may be an expert whittler. You can arrange for your children to spend some one-on-one time with him as he teaches this fine art to your children. Grandma may know how to cook the best peach pie in the world. Again, you can arrange for Grandma to teach any one of your children how to make this specialty. You may know how to knit, crochet, sew, build miniature train sets, make ice sculptures, play golf, ride horses or any number of special things. Teaching your children your special skills will delight them and make them very proud of you and themselves.

The trick to making this memorable for your children is to teach them your skills on an individual basis. No group encounters here. Just one adult with one child at a time. Then, watch your children shine!

136. Toast Time

On special family occasions, such as baptisms, confirmations, bar mitzvahs, birthdays or graduations, your family can begin celebrating with a special toast to the family "guest of honor."

You can keep special toasting glasses for "Toast Time," and these can be glasses which are used at no other time. You may wish to choose crystal glasses or pewter goblets. The glasses should be given a special place in your china cabinet or hutch. You may wish to serve champagne or Shirley Temples or sparkling cider in the toasting glasses.

The important thing is to honor family members with this symbolic toast. It will make your children feel very good about their achievements and about the achievements of others in the family. You will have to give the toasts when your children are young, but your children can give the toasts as they grow older. They will especially enjoy toasting you, and will undoubtedly pass this tradition on to their own families someday.

137. Baby's Tree

When a baby is born into your family, it is a cause for great celebration. This most miraculous event can be commemorated by having grandparents or other family members plant a tree in the baby's name.

It is probably a good idea to plant the tree in the front yard, just in case your family moves to a new home. That way, your family can still drive by your old home and visit the tree which was planted in your baby's honor. When visiting the tree, you can take the opportunity to describe to your child the love you felt when you first held him or her in your arms. You can quietly explain that this was a moment of immense joy for you. You may wish to have an inscribed plaque or other marker placed near the tree with your baby's name and birthdate on it. And, if you have more than one baby, a tree should be planted in honor of each of their births.

This living tree can serve to exemplify your growing love for your growing child. Flowers can be planted at its base on your child's birthday.

138. Bedtime

One of the special moments you will share with your children each day occurs at bedtime. When the lights are low and your voices are soft, you and your children can share a closeness and warmth which you will remember always. This is one of the best times for saying "I love you."

Your children may enjoy listening to you as you read them a story at night. Children love repetition, so don't be afraid to read the same story many times during the course of a year. Storytime is a great time for flannel p.j.'s, slippers, and soft music. And remember that children of all ages love bedtime stories, so even when your children become teenagers, they will still enjoy hearing you read or telling them stories.

Your children may also be comforted by having a picture of you on their nightstands, and a favorite stuffed animal nearby. And while your children are still babies, be sure to take a picture of them as they sleep.

139. Quiet Moments

Life can be very hectic at times, even for children. Every so often, you may wish to get away from it all with your children in order to spend a few quiet moments with each other and Mother Nature.

You may find that the greatest peace and tranquility comes from sitting near a stream with your children. Imagine, if you will, a warm day along a secluded stream . . . throwing pebbles into the water . . . and together, daydreaming about all of the wonderful things in your lives.

Quiet moments can also be found in the forest, and if you are lucky, you will spot a deer or two. These gentle creatures bring smiles to even the youngest faces. Your children may also enjoy spending quiet moments with you as you watch the sunset over the ocean. Wherever you may spend your quiet moments, your children are sure to enjoy having you all to themselves, without any interruptions from the outside world. These can be among the most precious moments you will spend together.

140. Eating Can Be Divine

Many families begin meals by saying "grace." Other families choose to begin meals with a moment of quiet meditation. Either way, these traditions serve to settle everyone down before they begin eating.

You may also wish to conclude each meal with a few words of "thanksgiving." Children can take turns on subsequent nights, ending the meal with a sentence or two about why they are grateful for the meal and their family. This serves as a nice way of concluding family meals in a formal manner.

You may also wish to have your children ask to be excused from the table after they have finished eating. This is a practice which will help them establish good table manners, which will be important throughout their lives.

141. It's Right to Write

You can help teach your children the protocol of writing letters and notes to family members and close friends by making this activity fun. You can do so by helping your children pick out special stationery, stickers, stamps and sealing wax.

Teaching your children how to write "Thank You" notes is one of the most important things you can do for them. You may wish to make it a family custom to acknowledge gifts by means of "Thank You" notes within twenty-four hours of receiving the gifts. This will set guidelines that your children will be able to live with, and remember, throughout their lives.

If parents, grandparents and relatives are asked, they may save these little notes and letters, and give them back to your children when they grow up. This kind of documentation can add immeasurably to your family's archives.

142. Charm 'em with Charms

Upon the birth of each of your children, you may wish to present your mother and mother-in-law with a gold charm, engraved with the name of their new grandchild.

These gold charms can be added to a gold charm bracelet which can be given to your mother and mother-in-law upon the birth of your first child.

As the years go by, your children will love to look at their grandmothers' gold charm bracelets. They will especially like finding the charms with their names on them.

Later in life, your children's grandmothers may choose to have each of the charms made into a pin or pendant, which can be presented to each of your children as a symbol of their grandparents' love. These will serve as gifts of great importance. Do not be surprised if your children continue this tradition when they have children of their own someday.

Conclusion

Children are life's most precious gift. They bring such love and laughter into our lives.

Today, we can preserve the happy and important times in our children's lives in many ways, such as by taking pictures, making audio recordings, using a video camera, writing in diaries, and putting together scrapbooks. Whatever our methods, the results will someday lead our children to look back on their early days with delight and appreciation.

Childhood days go by so quickly. Therefore, we hope that our suggestions will help you take advantage of the many "Memory Maker" opportunities you are about to experience, before they slip away. Traditions and family heritage are taught, and you have the power to teach your children well. We wish you great success as you endeavor to give your children memories to last a lifetime!